THE PS

The Lion Classic Bible Series

THE PSALMS

Ancient Poetry of the Spirit

Foreword by R.S. Thomas
Introduction by Lawrence Boadt
and F.F. Bruce

A LION BOOK

Published by
Lion Publishing plc
Sandy Lane West, Oxford, England
ISBN 0 7459 3805 1
Albatross Books Pty Ltd
PO Box 320, Sutherland, NSW 2232, Australia
ISBN 0 7324 1652 3

First edition 1997
10 9 8 7 6 5 4 3 2 1 0

A catalogue record for this book is available
from the British Library

Printed and bound in Great Britain by
Caledonian International Book Manufacturing, Glasgow

Contents

ACKNOWLEDGMENTS

The first part of the introduction has been reprinted from *Reading the Old Testament* by Lawrence Boadt © 1984 by The Missionary Society of St Paul the Apostle in the State of New York. Used by permission of Paulist Press.

'Hebrew Poetry' by F.F. Bruce has been selected from *A Dictionary of Biblical Tradition in English Literature*, edited by David Lyle Jeffrey, copyright © 1992 by permission of Wm B. Eerdmans Publishing Co.

The text of 'The Psalms in Literature' has been selected from *A Dictionary of Biblical Tradition in English Literature*, edited by David Lyle Jeffrey, copyright © 1992 by permission of Wm B. Eerdmans Publishing Co.

Parts 1–4 of 'The Psalms' have been taken from the Authorised Version of the Bible (The King James Bible), the rights in which are vested in the Crown, by permission of the Crown's Patentee, Cambridge University Press.

Parts 5 and 8 of 'The Psalms' have been taken from the Revised Standard Version of the Bible, copyright © 1946, 1952, 1971 by the Division of Christian Education of the National Council of the Churches of Christ in the USA.

Parts 6 and 7 of 'The Psalms' have been taken from the *New Jerusalem Bible* copyright © 1985 by permission of Darton, Longman and Todd Ltd and Doubleday and Company Inc.

Part 9 of 'The Psalms' has been taken from the Revised English Bible, copyright © 1989 by permission of Oxford and Cambridge University Presses.

Part 10 of 'The Psalms' has been taken fom the New Revised Standard Version of the Bible, copyright © 1989 by the Division of Christian Education of the National Council of the Churches of Christ in the USA.

Foreword

The only way to escape the curse of Babel is to become polyglot; an impossibility. Therefore we need translators. Where there are hidden riches in another language these endowed people will help us to share in them. In poetry the riches will be in the words and in the thoughts which the words convey.

The Psalms were Hebrew poetry, the expression of a nation's sorrow and exultation in its search for God. The meaning is the message, said Marshall McLuhan, so it is unwise to endeavour to separate meaning from form in poetry. The genius of the early translators of the Psalms into English enabled them to avoid this. Hence those verses which for so long have reverberated in the English psyche.

I rejoice that Lion Publishing has sought to remind us of these riches by making a generous selection from the King James Version, (although as an aged traditionalist I would have preferred the 1662 Prayer Book's rendering).

However, one virtue of this collection is that it reminds us of the existence of the Psalms in English and enables us to compare different versions of them. By dividing them into sections of praise, thanksgiving and lamentation we are shown where to turn to have our feelings eloquently expressed for us in our own attempts to find God and glorify him.

R.S. Thomas

INTRODUCTION

The Nature of the Book of Psalms

The psalms are 150 prayer-poems collected in a single book called the Psalter. All were probably intended to be sung or accompanied by music. But not all are alike. Many are brimming with joy and praise of God's goodness; others are filled with sorrow and lament and a spirit of contrition. Some are concerned with illness or bad fortune in life; some were used on weddings or other special occasions. But by having them all, we are able to see a depth and width of Israel's attitude towards Yahweh not present in any other book of the Bible. In Hebrew, the Book of Psalms is called *tehillim*, that is, 'Praises'. The name captures the meaning of these songs better than any other word. Even in psalms of deep sorrow and distress, the note of confidence and trust in God's goodness always comes through.

As they stand today, the 150 psalms do not seem to have any special subject order or theme development from one end to the other. It seems rather that the present book is made up from many smaller collections. For one thing, most psalms have a label at the beginning, which says 'of David', 'of Asaph', 'of Korah', or of others. These labels do not necessarily mean that the psalm was written *by* the man, but that it came from the collection under his name – in some cases, collected by him, or written by him, or just related to the office he held. Thus many David psalms probably mean 'from the royal collection', while Asaph psalms mean 'of the temple collection'.

For another thing, the psalms seem to be grouped in small collections. We have eight psalms of Korah together in Psalms 42–49, and eleven by Asaph in Psalms 73–83. Psalms 120–135 make up a group called the 'songs of ascent', perhaps used in processions or pilgrimages. Psalms 113–118 and 146–150 make up two 'Alleluia' collections. These collections in turn have been organized at some point into five 'books' of psalms so that the Psalter will match the Pentateuch[1] in shape. Thus we have the following five-part order in the present book of Psalms:

Book 1 Psalms 1–41, an early collection of Davidic hymns.

Book 2 Psalms 42–72, a northern collection of hymns.

Book 3 Psalms 73–89, a collection from the temple singers.

Book 4 Psalms 90–106, psalms from a royal collection, perhaps for New Year's.

Book 5 Psalms 107–150, a second and expanded Davidic royal collection.

Another piece of evidence for originally smaller collections is seen in the way some of the psalms from one 'book' repeat psalms from another book. Thus Psalm 14 matches Psalm 53, and Psalm 40:12–18 matches Psalm 70. The difference between the earlier and the later versions of each is the use of the name of God. Those in book 1 (Psalms 1–41) all use Yahweh, while those in book 2 (42–72) use Elohim, the word for God.

This is exactly the difference between the Yahwist and Elohist authors of the Pentateuch, and reflects a southern versus a northern kingdom outlook. The same psalms appeared in both kingdoms' collections when the two were combined into the present book, so that both examples were kept.

The Variety and Richness of the Psalms

To appreciate the beauty of the psalms, we must begin to read them for two things: the beauty of their language and images, and the unique thought and individuality of each. Since to read them all the way through at one sitting would be to get a bad case of spiritual indigestion, it is important to examine each psalm on its own merits. For this reason, scholars place a great deal of emphasis on the work of form criticism so that we can identify each psalm according to its special type. There are six major types recognized by most experts: (1) hymns of praise, (2) thanksgiving hymns, (3) individual laments, (4) community laments, (5) royal psalms honouring either Yahweh as king or the earthly king as his deputy, and (6) wisdom psalms.

Other smaller types can be seen and identified also. Psalm 45 is a wedding song; Psalms 15 and 24 are processional psalms for entering the temple; Psalms 93 and 95–99 are for a festival of Yahweh's kingship; Psalms 78, 105 and 106 recite the great historical deeds of salvation. By knowing the proper type of psalm, the reader gains a better focus for what the psalmist was trying to say and how the complete poem expresses that message.

Besides identifying a general category of psalm type for each psalm, it is important to understand its internal structure. Consider the example of a psalm of individual lament. Most of these psalms have a similar structure made up of the following elements:

(a) *an address to God*: 'Hear me, O God', often followed by praises

(b) *the lament itself*: the psalmist brings his complaint to God

(c) *confession of trust* in God and petition for relief

(d) *exclamation of certainty* that the psalmist's prayer has been or will be heard by God

(e) *the vow of praise*: the psalmist promises to declare God's praises to the community or to continue to praise him forever.

Other types of psalms have slightly different structures, but each different type follows its own special structure fairly closely. By paying attention to the differences as well as the common points, we learn a great deal about a psalm. For example, many people have wondered at the great emotional range in Psalm 22, in which the psalmist goes from the depth of despair to passages of absolute praise that God actually saved his life. If we recognize the lament structure in this psalm, we can see that the first twenty-two verses mix the psalmist's complaint with words of trust, while the last ten verses declare his absolute certainty that God has heard his prayer. The break between verses 22 and 23 is very sharp as a result, and many scholars have suggested that we should suppose that a priestly blessing was given over the worshipper at this moment in some temple service of healing. The praying psalmist receives the blessing and is moved to declare his confidence in God's healing, saving power.

The Liturgical Origins of the Psalms

This brings us to the burning issue in the modern study of the psalms as to whether they were primarily private prayer or public prayers of the temple. Of course, the temple had something to do with saving them, otherwise many would have been lost over the years as people came and went. But beyond this service as a library, there is good reason to believe that many, if not most, of the psalms originated in actual liturgical services. We know from later Jewish tradition, for example, that the Levitical priests recited the 'Hallel psalms' (Psalms 113–118) as the lambs were slaughtered on the feast of Passover. Indeed, themes of the exodus dominate many of these particular psalms (see Psalms 115 and 116). Were they composed originally for use in such a festival? Or were they only later adopted?

A similar use at Passover could account for Psalm 136 with its narration of the great saving deeds of Yahweh. At the same time, the autumn feasts of Rosh Hashana (New Year's) and of Booths may well have been specially dedicated to celebrating the kingship of Yahweh and his creation of the world, as well as the coronation and power of his delegate, the earthly king. Many psalms would ideally suit such a feast: Psalms 95–99 on Yahweh's kingship, or Psalms 29 and 47 on God's rule over creation, or Psalms 2 and 110 on the king's royal powers. This autumn feast or one like it may also have been a celebration of renewing the covenant God made with King David (2 Samuel 7). Psalms 89 and 132 would fit perfectly that idea.

Other possible festival or liturgical ceremonies include:

(1) *Purification and Sin Healing*. The themes in Psalms 81 and 106 stress the people's repentance for their long history of infidelity, while psalms such as 76 or 82 celebrate God as judge of the universe who will punish wicked nations for their evil. Psalm 50 may even be part of a day of atonement.

(2) *Pilgrimages*. Exodus 23:17 requires every male to go up for the three major feasts each year. The title 'song of ascents' in Psalms 120–134 has often been associated with the coming of groups to the temple for the big feasts. These psalms contain themes of looking

forward to the city or to what Yahweh has done, or remember the processions of the ark of the covenant.

(3) *Entrance Liturgies*. Psalms 15 and 24, in particular, seem to be sung at the gate of the temple by alternate choirs. One group on the outside asks permission to enter by singing God's praise; the second choir inside the gates demands that they be purified and worthy to enter. Then the gates open.

(4) *Zion Celebration Hymns*. Psalms 46, 48, 76, 87, 125 and others extol the temple and its special place in Jerusalem on the Mount of Zion. These praise the lasting promise of God to be with Israel and to make his home on Zion. It is hard to imagine that these could have been celebrated anywhere but on the temple grounds.

(5) *Wedding Songs*. Psalm 45 was probably sung on the king's wedding day.

(6) *Victory Songs*. Many songs are found in the Bible, although not always in the Psalter, that are clearly hymns of victory sung to Yahweh. Exodus 15 (the Song of Miriam) and Judges 5 (the Song of Deborah) are certainly such. Psalms 66 and 68 may also be of this type.

(7) *Hymns for the King*. Special royal songs may well have played a major part in ceremonies at times of battles or on the king's birthday when the people prayed for his health and well-being. Psalms 20, 21, 60, 61 and 72 may belong to such a category.

Other signs that the psalms were used primarily in the temple for public worship can be found in the directions for musical accompaniment that head many psalms. Psalm 4, as an example, begins with the note, 'With stringed instruments'. Psalm 8 is to be played upon 'the gittith'. Psalm 45 is to be sung 'according to the tune of "The Lilies", a love song'. Musical accompaniment was very important to temple services, as the biblical descriptions make clear. 1 Chronicles 16 lists the temple singers who joined Asaph in singing while the ark was carried to Jerusalem. 1 Chronicles 25 gives a detailed list of temple musical personnel. Concretely, in 2 Chronicles 5:13, the temple singers sing a verse that looks as though it is part of Psalm 136: 'Give thanks to the Lord for he is good, his mercy endures forever.' Then, too, many of the psalms mention aspects of worship that are to be performed while the words are being sung. Processions are mentioned in Psalms 42, 68 and 132, and praying in the temple itself in Psalms 5:7 and 26:6–7. All of this makes a strong case for the primary origin of the psalms in public worship.

Personal Piety and the Psalms

Despite their public use, most of the psalms also contain a very personal note, including strong emotions and personal concerns that express the psalmist's anguish or great joy. Quite possibly any single psalm began in the personal prayer of someone either in distress or feeling thankful, and was so appreciated and liked that it was treasured and used by all, much as modern Christians love the prayer of St Francis of Assisi for peace, or have recited the famous 'Breastplate Prayer of St Patrick' down through the ages. The personal songs were taken up and modified for congregational use. This would be particularly true of the individual laments.

The deepest insight into the religious prayer of an ancient Israelite comes from the ways the psalmists address God. In the psalms, certain qualities of Yahweh are mentioned over and over again. Among the most important of these are:

(1) *God is holy.* He is addressed as the 'Holy One of Israel' in Psalms 71:22 and 78:41. This signifies Israel's belief that God was not one of us, but apart from and above human life, and in him alone was the fulness of life and power. Another example is Psalm 89:18 (New Jerusalem Bible):

> for to Yahweh belongs our shield, to the Holy One of Israel
> our king.

(2) *God is greater than all gods.* The mention of other gods does not mean that Israel was not truly monotheist in its faith. Psalms that affirm the greatness of God are engaged in a debate with the pagans who believe in many gods, and so they use the language of contrast. Psalm 89 certainly doesn't consider Yahweh to be only one god among many when it says:

Who in the skies can compare with Yahweh? Who among the sons of god can rival him?

The answer is obvious: there is no being at all like Yahweh!

(3) *God is eternal*. Yahweh is not like us humans. He has been and will be the enduring source of life and hope:

Before the mountains were brought forth or the earth and the world were born, from age to age you are God. (Psalm 90:2, Revised English Bible)

God's *name* also endures forever as the power that the psalmist calls upon in times of trouble. (Psalm 54:1; 135:13)

(4) *God is a rock and fortress to defend us*. The psalms refer to God as a rock or a fortress or a refuge to signify his unchanging fidelity and loving protection. One of the most moving passages in the Book of Psalms is the opening of Psalm 18:

'Yahweh is my rock and my fortress, my deliverer is my God. I take refuge in him, my rock, my shield, my saving strength, my stronghold, my place of refuge'. (Psalm 18:2, New Jerusalem Bible)

Protection and refuge can also be tender and gentle in the theology of the psalmists:

He that dwelleth in the secret place of the most High shall abide under the shadow of the Almighty. I will say of the Lord, He is my refuge and my fortress: my God; in him will I trust. (Psalm 91:1–2, King James Version)

(5) *God is a redeemer*. Israel calls upon Yahweh to deliver them as he once delivered their ancestors at the Red Sea. But this time it could be from sickness, the snares of enemies, or death:

With thy faithful help rescue me from sinking in the mire; let me be delivered from my enemies and from the deep waters... Hide not thy face from thy servant; for I am in distress, make haste to answer me. Draw near to me, redeem me, set me free because of my enemies! (Psalm 69:14–18, Revised Standard Version)

(6) *God is compassionate and merciful.* The Hebrew concept of *hesed* is more than just mercy; it contains the idea of steadfast love, loyalty and kindness as well. All things reveal this kindly face of God: 'The earth, O Lord, is full of your *hesed*' (Psalm 119:64, New Revised Standard Version). Psalm 136 adds after each verse the refrain, 'for his *hesed* endures for ever'. It is the heart of the covenant relationship between Israel and Yahweh:

Satisfy us at daybreak with your *hesed*, that we may sing for joy and be glad all our days. (Psalm 90:14, Revised English Bible)

(7) *God is just, and upright.* Above all else God is not wicked and deceitful as humans are. He can be trusted because he upholds what is right:

Enter not into judgment with thy servant: for no man living is righteous before thee. (Psalm 143:2, Revised Standard Version)

Above all, God is concerned with justice for the poor and oppressed:

Happy is he that hath the God of Jacob for his help, whose hope is in the Lord his God…: Which executeth judgment for the oppressed: which giveth food to the hungry. The Lord looseth the prisoners: The Lord openeth the eyes of the blind: the Lord raiseth them that are bowed down: the Lord loveth the righteous: The Lord preserveth the strangers; he relieveth the fatherless and widow: but the way of the wicked he turneth upside down. (Psalm 146:5–9, King James Version)

There are many other ways to discover the religious feelings of the Israelites through the psalms. For example, the important problem questions of future hope, faith, sin and forgiveness, and divine providence could be examined. The importance of certain themes known from the prophets and the Pentateuch might be studied as they appear in the prayers of the psalms: the exodus, the 'glory' (*kabod*) of God, the divine 'name', or the concern with the poor and powerless (*anawim*). A whole book in its own right would need to be devoted to these ideas in order to do them justice. But in the end, the understanding of these sides of the biblical faith would lead us straight back to the titles of Yahweh above.

The psalmists loved to speak of God under endless descriptive names: not just 'rock', 'fortress', 'stronghold', 'saviour', and 'redeemer', but also in dozens of others, including, 'The Mighty One', the 'Most High', 'my inheritance', 'my portion', 'my cup', 'king', and 'judge of the earth'. In reading the psalms, it is important to be aware of the divine titles and the rich language that Israel developed to express the wonderful sense of God's mysterious goodness that they had experienced in so many ways in all aspects of their lives.

Sickness and Tragedy in the Psalms

Psalms 6, 30, 32, 38, 39, 41 and 88 are all good examples of psalms directed to a time of personal sickness. God seemed to allow sickness by turning away his face (Psalm 30:8), or even by actually willing it – see also 2 Samuel 12:15 (the case of David's child by Bathsheba), or 1 Samuel 16:14 (the case of Saul). An Israelite had several places to turn in sickness. Sirach 38:1 shows that natural healing by poultices and medicines was often expected. But where no remedy could be found, the sick person could turn to God in prayer. (Isaiah 38 gives us a very clear picture of King Hezekiah praying to God for healing.)

Prayer and medical knowledge worked hand in hand and priests often doubled as medical functionaries. Leviticus 14 and 15 gives various directions for the priestly treatment of leprosy, open sores and skin eruptions. There may even be reflections of special healing services performed at the temple present in the psalms; see Psalms 26:6 and 73:13 as samples.

Another concern that faced the psalmists was the ever-present danger from evil spirits or demons that caused sickness and death. The people of other ancient nations had elaborate rituals for driving off demons and evil spirits, and saying the proper incantations and prayers to prevent these beings from having power over a person. But in biblical thought, no demons can have power unless Yahweh lets them, so that psalms of persons in distress often combine a prayer of piety towards Yahweh with pleas against evil demons or forces outside the person. The faithful confess their own sins and claim their faithfulness in important matters so that God will have mercy on them and turn the evil back on the spirits or on an enemy. See examples such as Psalms 5:8–11, 6:1–11, 10:1–15, 17:10–15 and many others.

In Christian tradition, special place has been given to the so-called 'Penitential Psalms' (Psalms 6, 32, 38, 51, 102, 130 and 143), which express a strong personal note of penitence for sins and a heartfelt plea for mercy. Psalm 51 is the greatest of these, and reaches a particularly high note of humility in which God's mercy is readily praised as totally and freely given:

> Have mercy on me, O God, according to thy steadfast love;
> according to thy abundant mercy blot out my transgressions.
> (Psalm 51:1, Revised Standard Version)

No matter how low a person gets, God's faithful and compassionate love is always ready to restore and bring joy to his or her life:

> Restore to me the joy of thy salvation, and uphold me with
> a willing spirit. (Psalm 51:12)

Lawrence Boadt

Hebrew Poetry

Hebrew poetry is characterized by certain rhythmical patterns which can to a large extent be reproduced in translation. There is rhythm of sound, which is mainly based on a regular sequence of stressed syllables; there is rhythm of sense, which takes the form of 'parallelism'. That is to say, what is essentially the same idea is expressed twice over in parallel clauses; the idea is the same, but the words are different.

There are three main varieties of parallelism: complete, incomplete, and step.

Complete parallelism. Here each significant word in one line has its counterpart in another. The parallelism may be synonymous:

> Adah and Zillah, hear my voice;
> ye wives of Lamech, hearken unto my speech.
> (Genesis 4:23; King James Version)

It may be antithetic:

> They will crumple and fall,
>   while we stand upright and firm.
> (Psalm 20:8; New Jerusalem Bible)

Or it may be emblematic, where the situation in one line is compared to the situation in the adjoining line:

> Like as a father pitieth his children,
>   so the Lord pitieth them that fear him.
> (Psalm 103:13; King James Version)

Sometimes the parallelism is more elaborate, and consists in the balancing of groups of lines rather than of single lines. A good example is provided by Psalm 27:1:

> The Lord is my light and my salvation;
>   whom shall I fear?
> the Lord is the strength of my life;
>   of whom shall I be afraid? (King James Version)

This pattern, in which lines of three and two stressed syllables alternate, is often called the 'dirge' rhythm because it is so characteristic of the book of Lamentations, but the example just quoted shows that it can also serve as the vehicle of joyful praise.

Incomplete parallelism. Sometimes one word in a line has no counterpart in the parallel line. Consider, for example, Psalm 40:2:

> He brought me up also out of an horrible pit,
>   out of the miry clay. (King James Version)

Here there is no verb in the second line; it is understood from the first line. The result is again an alternation of three and two stressed syllables. But sometimes an additional stressed syllable will be provided in the second line to preserve the same rhythm as in the first line. Where no additional stressed syllable is supplied, we have incomplete parallelism *without compensation;* where one is supplied, we have incomplete parallelism *with compensation.* Thus Psalm 1:5 runs:

> Therefore the wicked will not stand in the judgment,
> nor sinners in the congregation of the righteous.
> (New Revised Standard Version)

Here, as in Psalm 40:2, the verb is lacking in the second line, but now the number of stressed syllables is made up by the use of a heavier phrase, 'the congregation of the righteous,' in the second line as the counterpart of 'the judgment' in the preceding line. Sometimes there is even less parallelism of meaning and correspondingly more compensation in the supply of stressed syllables, until the point is reached where we have all compensation and no real parallelism. An example of this formal parallelism, as it has been called, comes in Psalm 27:6:

> And now shall mine head be lifted up
> above mine enemies round about me. (King James Version)

There are three stressed syllables in each line, but no single word in the one line has a sense counterpart in the other.

Step parallelism. Occasionally part of one line is repeated in the next, and becomes the starting point for a further step; this process may be repeated from line to line. Psalm 29:1, 2 presents a good example of this:

> Give Yahweh his due, sons of God,
> give Yahweh his due of glory and strength,
> give Yahweh the glory due to his name,
> adore Yahweh in the splendour of holiness.
> (New Jerusalem Bible)

Here the step parallelism is seen in the repeated 'give Yahweh' of the first three lines; lines 3 and 4 stand in complete synonymous parallelism the one to the other. Another example is Psalm 92:9:

> For, lo, thine enemies, O Lord,
> for, lo, thine enemies shall perish;
> all the workers of iniquity shall be scattered.
> (King James Version)

Lines 1 and 2 show step parallelism; lines 2 and 3 show complete synonymous parallelism.

Hebrew poetry sometimes exhibits strophic structure. One sign of this is the recurrence of a refrain. The recurring refrain of Psalms 42 and 43 (originally a single psalm) marks the end of three strophes, at verses 5 and 11 of Psalm 42 and verse 5 of Psalm 43. A strophic arrangement is indicated in Psalm 46:7, 11 by the refrain:

> The Lord of hosts is with us;
> the God of Jacob is our refuge
> (King James Version) –

but verses 1–7 probably comprised two strophes, with their dividing point marked by 'Selah' at the end of verse 3 (where the refrain was originally sung too). Psalm 80 is divided into four strophes by the refrain 'God, restore us...' (or 'God of Hosts, turn to us...') in verses 3, 7, 14, and 19 (Revised English Bible). The second part of Psalm 24 shows a more involved strophic pattern, with the repeated command 'Lift up your heads, O ye gates!' and the question 'Who is this King of glory?' (with response) (Revised Standard Version).

Strophic arrangement is also involved in certain acrostic poems. The most outstanding acrostic scheme is that of Psalm 119, whose twenty-two sections are formal strophes, corresponding to the twenty-two letters of the Hebrew alphabet, each of the eight sentences in the first section beginning with the first letter, and so on to the eight sentences of the last section, each of which begins with the twenty-second letter.

Numerous attempts have been made in English to capture the 'Hebraic' quality of biblical poetry. Most have been as unsuccessful in this respect as the translation of the Psalms (1586; 1599) by Sir Philip

Sidney and the Countess of Pembroke. Despite the fact that John Donne labelled the 'Sydnean Psalmes' an important achievement, the best rendering was much closer to hand.

The influence of Hebrew poetry first enters English literary tradition in a significant way with the 1611 'Authorized' translation. The forty-seven translators working under the auspices of King James may have had less intention to capture in English the prose rhythms and parallelism of Hebrew poetry with which they are credited; however, subsequent understanding of Hebrew verse has suggested that certain corresponding features of Renaissance English prosody and a strong intuitive feeling for the Hebrew of the Psalms particularly combined to make the King James Version a remarkable access into the character of Hebrew verse. A similar poetic intuition is reflected in the canon of George Herbert, whose 'Antiphon' not only conflates lines from a number of Psalms, but in its 'focusing parallelism' can be seen as a direct response to 'the dynamics of biblical poetry and its relation to the life of the Spirit'.[2]

In the 18th century when the King James Version had already wrought an enormous influence on English prosody generally, Bishop Robert Lowth did an extended analysis of Hebrew poetry in his *Lectures on the Sacred Poetry of the Hebrews (De Sacra Poesi Hebraeorum)*, published in 1753. This volume had an immediate impact on Christopher Smart, among others, whose brilliant, structurally and conceptually intricate *Song to David* (1763) and often powerfully rhythmic exercise in the Hebrew 'Let' / 'For' sequence (discussed by Lowth), the *Jubilate Agno* (1759–63), are among the most innovative 18th-century responses to the Bible. Lowth had noted that the crowding of metaphors, while a violation of Aristotle's edicts about perspicuity, was a natural expression of oriental style, in which 'the language of poetry... [is] wholly distinct from that of common life'. Lowth also established that prophetic poetry consisted of the accumulation of individual distichs and in this respect his work may have had a significant influence on William Blake's early prophecies.

Byron's collection of short poems, *Hebrew Melodies* (1815), are on scriptural subjects (e.g., 'The Destruction of Sennacherib'), and some were arranged to traditional Hebrew melodies by I. Nathan. Later in the 19th century Robert Browning was interested enough in

Hebrew poetry to pursue rabbinical literature for analysis of biblical tradition and expression. His 'Rabbi Ben Ezra' and 'Jochanan Hakkadosh' are efforts to create the feel of Hebrew prose rhythms, however, rather than the actual qualities of Hebrew poetry.

Despite Arnold's having cast aspersions on 'Hebraism' in culture generally and literature particularly (*Culture and Anarchy*, 1869), interest in the qualities of Hebrew biblical poetry persisted into the 20th century, influencing not only Israeli poets such as Tavia Rubner but also Jewish poets writing in English such as A.M. Klein, whose *Hitleriad* and *Psalter of Avram Hakni* (1944) capture much of the flavour of the poetry of wisdom literature, favouring especially incomplete or verb–carry-over parallelisms.

F.F. Bruce

Note

1. The first five books of the Bible (Genesis, Exodus, Leviticus, Numbers and Deuteronomy), traditionally referred to as the Five Books of Moses.
2. R. Alter, *The Art of Biblical Poetry*, 1985, p. 210.

THE PSALMS IN LITERATURE

Quotations and Images

Quotations and Images

Cup Runneth Over

'My cup runneth over' (Psalm 23:5) signifies that the speaker enjoys an abundance of good fortune. He recounts the blessings he has received from God and sums them up in these words. Their influence appears repeatedly in English literature; for example, 'the cup of his [Jeremy's] joy was full' (H. Walpole, *Jeremy and Hamlet*, 11.1). But perhaps even more often the figure denotes an excess of sorrow or anger; for example, 'the cup of her indignation ran over' (A. Trollope, *Barchester Towers*, chapter 11); 'This was all that was wanted to make poor Tom's cup of bitterness run over' (W.M. Thackeray, *The Newcomes*, chapter 2).

F.F. Bruce
University of Manchester

De Profundis

The opening words of Vulgate Psalm 129:1 are '*De profundis clamavi, ad te, Domine.*' In the corresponding Psalm 130, the King James Version reads, 'Out of the depths have I cried unto thee, O Lord.'

Various effective medieval English translations notwithstanding, the text receives some of its richest adaptation in the Renaissance. John Skelton uses the text of Psalm 130:1 paradoxically, together with its proper antiphon, found in the Office of the Dead ('Phyllyp Sparowe'):

> Si in i qui ta tes,
> Alas, I was evyll at ease!
> De profun dis cla ma vi,
> Whan I sawe my sparowe dye!

Thomas Campion's elegant air is perhaps unsurpassed in poetic translation in the period. It begins:

> Out of my soules deapth to thee my cryes haue sounded
> Let thine eares my plaints receiue, on iust feare grounded

Lord, should'st thou weigh our faults,
who's not confounded?

But the long poem of George Gascoigne (circa 1575) is almost equal
to it in vigour. Entitled '*De Profundis*', it renders in colourful 16th-
century language the whole of Psalm 130, affirming the covenant
promise of God to Israel, here typologically also the Christian elect:

From depth of dole wherein my soul doth dwell,
From heavy heart which harbours in my breast,
From troubled sprite which seldom taketh rest,
From hope of heaven, from dread of darksome hell,
O gracious God, to thee I cry and yell,
My God, my Lord, my lovely Lord alone,
To thee I call, to thee I make my moan…

John Donne, whose meditations and psalms resonate the *de profundis*
theme, employs in his 'Lamentations of Jeremy' translations a
collation of Psalm 130:1 with Lamentations 3:55: 'I called Lord, upon
thy name, / Out of the pit…'

Robert Browning uses the traditional context of Psalm 130 in *The
Ring and the Book* (1.1318–19). Count Guido Franceschini, having
confessed to the murder of his wife, is about to be executed when the
'black fellowship' (of chaplains) 'intone the lamentable psalm, "Out of
the deeps, Lord, have I cried to thee!"'. It is invoked in a similar context
by Melville in *Clarel* (2.25.190): 'Her God her deprofundis roll.'

In Søren Kierkegaard's *Journals*, the theme becomes to some
extent a preoccupation. Speaking of the sufferings that each person
has to endure to improve the lot of all mankind, Kierkegaard claims
that individuals must be sacrificed to be a 'little dash of cinnamon' in
God's recipe for divine Providence. 'Painful it is to be sacrificed in this
manner – to be a little dash of cinnamon!' Each person so sacrificed
learns to sing a

deprofundis – that God is love…
Underneath, supporting, as it were,
all these sopranos as the bass part
does, [and] sounds the *deprofundis* from
the sacrificed ones: God is love.

Following Kierkegaard, Lev Shestov takes the *'de profundis'* into philosophic-theological inquiry in his essay entitled *'De Profundis'*.

The title given to Oscar Wilde's *'Epistola: in Carcere et Vinculis'* by his editor Robert Ross, *De Profundis*, does not reflect a penitential intent. Wilde seems rather to have created his own religion from a hell within himself, reflected in the external geography of the place where he was imprisoned. To be released, he has to deliver himself from bitter feelings much, as he imagines, like those of Dante in the *Inferno*. In the midst of a threatening flood, the parishioners in Dorothy Sayers' *The Nine Tailors* (3.3) cry for help in the *Book of Common Prayer* version, 'Out of the deep, O Lord, out of the deep' as the sluice begins to give way.

Ernest N. Kaulbach
University of Texas, Austin

Deep Calleth unto Deep

Etymologically and mythologically this deep (Psalm 42:7) has affinities with a symbolically related set of primordial sea monsters, and some connection is intended also with the deep upon the face of which darkness lay at the creation (Genesis 1:2) and the deep which God will bring upon wicked Tyre (Ezekiel 26:19). King James Version's 'waterspouts' is improved upon by Revised Standard Version's 'cataracts', which give the watery ferment a clearer context.

A mythologized 'deep' (often again in combination with 'dark') is in Milton's *Paradise Lost* the abode of the fallen angels, meant to reflect both the abysses of their own nothingness and the hoary unreality which God's creativity has not touched. Biblical resonances of this deep help to damn the devils, and in Pope's *Dunciad* a metamorphosed version of it gives weight to the dunces' selfdamnation. In Traherne the unfulfilled heart can be 'a deep profound Abyss' ('Desire,' 22).

In Vaughan's 'Abels Blood' the blood of Abel which cries out in Genesis 4:10 leads up to the blood of all those murdered by their fellow humans, a

> ...deep, wide sea of blood?
> A sea, whose lowd wave cannot sleep,
> But *Deep* still calleth unto *deep*...

And in Hopkins' 'Nondum' Nondum likens mankind's searching for God (to which 'not yet' is the answer) to an abyss where 'Deep calls to deep and blackest night / Giddies the soul with blinding daze...'

Whittier, in 'Massachusetts to Virginia', characterizes the moral outrage over the re-taking of an escaped Southern slave in Boston as

The voice of Massachusetts! Of her free sons and daughters
Deep calling unto deep aloud, the sound of many waters!
Against the burden of that voice what tyrant power shall stand?
No fetters in the Bay State! No slave upon her land!

Emerson's *Nature* (section 8), on the other hand, uses the deep calling as a metaphor for his notion of transcendental integration with self and nature:

The reason why the world lacks unity... is, because man is disunited with himself... In the uttermost meaning of the words, thought is devout, and devotion thought. Deep calleth unto deep.

Richard Schell
Laurentian University

Dirige

The term *Dirige* is derived from Vulgate Psalm 5:9 and Psalm 5:8 ('*Dirige, Domine Deus meus, in conspectu tuo viam meam*' ['Direct, O Lord my God, my way in your sight']). In Christian liturgy, Psalm 5:8 was used as the first antiphon in the first Nocturn of Matins in the Office of the Dead. The first word, *Dirige*, came to signify the recitation of Matins for the souls of the dead and ultimately the recitation of the entire Office of the Dead. It was also used to signify one's obligation to pray for the dead, as in the C-text of Langland's *Piers Plowman* (4.467–68): 'Prestes and persons . placebo and dirige, / Here sauter and here seuene psalmis . for alle synful preyen' ('Priests and parsons pray *placebo* and *dirige* / Their psalter and their seven psalms for all the sinful').

With the loss of a syllable, *Dirige* became *dirge*, as in Sidney's '"Love is Dead": Let Dirge be sung, / and trentals rightly read.'

The refrain at the end of each stanza, 'Good Lord, deliver us', imitates the Litany in the *Book of Common Prayer*, and parallels the Latin Litany ('*Libera nos, Domine*') said over the grave of the deceased in the liturgical ceremonies of graveside burial. The later poetry of Alexander Pope conserves the liturgical sense of the word ('Nor hollow'd dirge be muttered o'er thy tomb' ['Elegy,' 67]; cf. 'Chaucer: January and May,' 146–47, 221). Spenser, satirizing Roman Catholic practices, refers to 'their dirges, their trentals, / and their shrifts' ('Prosopopoia: or Mother Hubbard's Tale,' 452).

For the transferred sense of a song sung at the burial or commemoration of the dead, see Shelley's 'Ode to the West Wind' ('Thou dirge / Of the dying year'); Thomas Gray's 'Elegy Written in a Country Churchyard' ('The next with dirges due in sad array / Slow through the church-way path we saw him borne'); Melville's *Clare* ('with litany or dirge they wend'); and Eliot's note to line 74 of *The Waste Land*.

Ernest N. Kaulbach
University of Texas, Austin

Four Daughters of God

The Daughters or Graces of God are said to be Truth, Righteousness (Justice), Mercy, and Peace – allegorical characters whose origin is in the words of Psalm 85:10, 'Mercy and truth are met together; righteousness and peace have kissed each other.' In Jewish tradition these virtues were seen as the four standards of the throne of God (see L. Ginzberg, *Legends of the Jews*, 6.82). Christian development of the motif owes largely to the commentaries of Hugh of St Victor and the sermons of St Bernard of Clairvaux.

In later medieval literature the narrative of the four daughters has many variations. In general, it consists of debate (sometimes in the presence of God in heaven) about the wisdom of creating humanity and about the propriety of strict justice or mercy for the fallen human race. Justice and Truth appear for the prosecution, representing the old Law, while Mercy speaks for the defence, and Peace presides over their reconciliation when Mercy prevails.

In many English texts the scene is set at some point well after the creation, for example, just before the Annunciation (as in the

Ludus Coventriae and most other literary and iconographic occurrences) or immediately after the death of Christ (as in *Piers Plowman*). In *The Castle of Perseverance* the debate occurs after the death of Humanum Genus, who is then admitted to heaven. In a version known as *Processus Belial (The Devil's Lawsuit)*, Belial summons Justice and Truth to his aid, and the Virgin calls on Mercy and Peace. In the late 16th-century fragment *Processus Satanae*, God himself calls Mercy and Peace to plead against Justice and Verite.

The virtues appear with some frequency in books of hours, generally in the Annunciation section. The colours of their clothes are specified in the map to *The Castle of Perseverance*: Mercy wears white, Justice red, Truth 'sad green', and Peace black.

Other iconographic conventions appear with some frequency. Justice is generally represented with scales or a sword; Peace with a palm, inverted torch, or truncated sword; Truth with a carpenter's square or tables of the Law; and Mercy with a box of ointment. The virtues are not always represented as female: in *Mankind* Mercy and Truth are male.

The debate of the Four Daughters occurs in a variety of Middle English texts, including *Cursor Mundi* (1.9517–52); *Gesta Romanorum* (no. 55); Grosseteste's *Castel of Love*, a translation of *Chasteau D'Amour* (1275); *The Court of Sapience* (book 1); Langland's *Piers Plowman* (B.18; C.21); *Castel of Perseverance* (3130); *Mankind* (832–82); *Ludus Coventriae* (97–103).

The allegory persisted through the Renaissance and even into minor Stuart poetry. There are possible echoes in the court scene in Shakespeare's *The Merchant of Venice* (4.1) and in Milton's *Paradise Lost* (3.132–34). But while the relationship of Justice to Mercy continues to have currency in literary tradition well after the 17th century, the elaborated allegory of the four virtues does not.

Michael Murphy
Brooklyn College, City University of New York

Green Pastures

'He maketh me to lie down in green pastures' (Psalm 23:2) is one of the best-known pastoral images of God's provident care for his people. As such it is often used ironically, as in Shakespeare's *Henry V*, when at the reporting of Falstaff's death the tavern hostess, who would believe him gathered into 'Arthur's bosom,' says of his last words that "a babbled of green fields' (2.3.17). In Coleridge's *The Wanderings of Cain* the ghost of Abel cries out to Cain in bitterness that he has been bereft of the delights of feeding his 'flocks in green pastures by the side of quiet rivers'. In an incidental allusion to the Psalm John Galsworthy describes the habitat of the Forsythes as 'green pastures' (*In Chancery*, 3.10). Menken, in similar fashion, argues that a college degree 'lifts [a young person] over a definite fence, and maketh him to lie down in greener pastures' (*A Menken Crestomathy*, 314). Marc Connelly's *The Green Pastures* (1929) is a slapstick comedy based on Roark Bradford's stories of African-American interpretation of biblical lore.

David L. Jeffrey
University of Ottawa

Hart

'As the hart panteth after the water brooks, so panteth my soul after thee, O God' (Psalm 42:1). The hart is the male (the hind or doe being the female) of this species of 'clean' animals (Deuteronomy 12:15). In the Yalqut annotation of Psalm 42:2 the hart is designated as the most pious of all animals, since it digs in the earth for water with its antlers, praying to God, and is rewarded with springs of living water rising from the desert sands, enough for itself and other creatures.

In *Beowulf* the pool where the hero's successful conflict with Grendel's dam takes place is said to be so full of serpents that a hart would rather face the hunters' dogs than leap in – a possibly ironic allusion to another tradition concerning the hart. According to medieval bestiaries, the hart is able to smell out a snake in its den and then stamp it to death; as such it is likened to Christ, who hunts out the Serpent, Satan, to destroy him (e.g., *De Bestiis et Aliis Rebus*, Patrologia Latina, 176). Typically, however, the hart is symbolic of the human soul, as in Chaucer's *Book of the Duchess*, where the Emperor Octavyen's harthunting concludes simultaneously with the successful 'heart-hunt' of the psychopharmical dialogue between the grieving Black Knight and Chaucer's persona. In his adaptation of 'the Lamentations of Jeremy' Donne speaks of the desolate state of Jerusalem in words close to his text (Lamentations 1:6):

> From Sion's daughter all beauty gone,
> Like Harts, which seek for Pasture, and find none,
> Her Princes are, and now before the foe
> Which still pursues them, without strength they go. (21–24)

These associations are compounded in romance literature by Celtic borrowings, in which, however, the hart may still be symbolic of the soul (e.g., *Erec et Enide, Mabinogion*).

In later literature allusions to the well-known *incipit* to Psalm 42 take a wide variety of verbal forms. The image of the exhausted soul 'Like as the hart desires the brook / In summer heat's extream degree' (Christopher Smart's translation) appealed to the psychologically distressed William Cowper, among whose best-known lines are:

> I was a stricken deer, that left the herd
> Long since; with many an arrow deep infixt
> My panting side was charged when I withdrew
> To seek a tranquil death in distant shades.
> There was I found by one who had himself
> Been hurt by the archers. (*The Task*, 3.108–13)

This type of loose association of the two conventional symbols – the hart as the soul and the hart as Christ – is reduced to a reference to the exhausted human soul alone with itself in Byron's *Manfred*:

> We can number
> How few, how less than few, wherein the soul
> Forbears to 'pant for death' and yet draws back
> As from a stream in winter. (2.2.266–69)

In Dickens' *Dombey and Son* Cuttle confusedly mis-remembers the text of Psalm 42: 'The wery planks she walked on was as high esteemed by Wal'r as the waterbrooks is by the hart which never rejoices.'

David L. Jeffrey
University of Ottawa

He that Diggeth a Pit

Six times in the Old Testament and once in the book of Sirach the belief in a just recoil upon the wicked is expressed as the evildoer's falling into the very pit he had dug to destroy another; often this image is paired with that of a net set to snare another and, in Proverbs, Ecclesiastes, and Sirach, of a stone set or thrown to harm him, but harming the evildoer instead (Psalms 7:14–16; 9:15–16; 35:7–8; 57:6; Proverbs 26:27; Ecclesiastes 10:8–9; and Sirach 27:28–30).

The late 16th-century biblical 'comedy' *Queen Esther and Proud Haman* concludes with Haman's being dragged off to the gallows and with Ahasuerus' allusion to evildoers who, having dug a pit for others, fall into it themselves. Marlowe uses the same pit image twice. In *The Massacre at Paris*, King Henry III, knowing that the Duke of Guise intends his overthrow and death, hires three murderers, then urges: 'Come, Guise, and see thy traitorous guile outreached, / And perish in the pit thou mad'st for me' (20.32–33). The association of this image with the traitor Judas and the other Jews who participated in the Crucifixion, and with financial fraud, may have recommended this means for the demise of the traitor and usurer in *The Jew of Malta*. Barabas plans to betray his allies so that their leader will fall 'into a deep pit past recovery' where he will burn to death in a cauldron. Instead, the trap is sprung on Barabas himself so that he perishes in a 'Cauldron placed in a pit'.

George Herbert sets Psalm 7 into verse (as had Sidney) and alludes to related stone images three times in other pieces. Twice he refers to the cast stone of Sirach 27:28. In 'Charms and Knots' he notes: 'Who by aspersions throw a stone / At th' head of others, hit their own' (9–10). In *A Priest to the Temple*, Herbert describes the parson as immune to others' scorn, either ignoring it, 'shewing that reproaches touch him no more, than a stone thrown against heaven', or reminding the 'contemner, Alas, why do you thus? you hurt your selfe, not me; he that throws a stone at another, hits himselfe' (chapter 28). Once, in 'Outlandish Proverbs', Herbert uses the other stone image associated with the pit, for example, in Ecclesiastes 10:9: 'Whoso removeth stones shall be hurt therewith.' Herbert writes: 'Who remove stones, bruise their fingers' (no. 40).

Stevenson invokes the image of pit and snare twice in his *New Arabian Nights*, to adumbrate and to clarify the climax. The diabolical, nameless President of the Suicide Club is the villain of the first, three-instalment tale. In the second instalment, he frames a young man for murder; the pit and snare allusions occur in a friend's words of sympathy for the youth. In the third instalment, the President plans to murder the Prince of Bohemia and digs a secret grave for him. Prince Florizel, however, surprises his plot; before slaying him in a duel, the prince declares, '[Y]ou have laid your last snare and your own feet are taken in it… And the grave you had dug for me this afternoon shall serve, in God's almighty providence, to hide your own just doom.'

When Sherlock Holmes discovers the corpse of the murderer Grimesby Roylott, killed by the swamp adder he had meant to kill his stepdaughter, Doyle has his detective observe, 'Violence does, in truth, recoil upon the violent, and the schemer falls into the pit which he digs for another' ('The Case of the Speckled Band').

At least three 20th-century novels use the pit image. In Dorothy Sayers' *The Documents in the Case* (1930), the adulterous Margaret Harrison writes to her lover, pretending that her husband's death was the accidental result of his experimenting with mushrooms, which she compares to 'digging a pit for himself to fall into, like the wicked man in the Bible' (Document 46). Her own correspondence with her lover, however, is the pit she dug for herself, for it is the evidence of her inciting him to murder.

Patricia Wentworth's *Lonesome Road* (1939) is informed by the image, for two attempts at murder recall the pit, the second sustaining the image through three chapters. Chapter 35 concludes with the first half of the verse echoing in the main character's thoughts; at the end of chapter 38 the would-be murderer backs into the well which he had uncovered in order to kill someone else, and the chapter concludes, 'The verse which Rachel had not been able to finish finished itself: They have digged a pit and fallen into it themselves.'

The final book of J.R.R. Tolkien's Middle-Earth trilogy features literal pits: the orcs besieging Gondor dig deep trenches which they fill with fire; then, however, the Roherrim surprise the orcs from

THE PSALMS IN LITERATURE

behind, 'hewing, slaying, driving their foes into the fire-pits' (*The Return of the King*, chapter 6).

Catherine Brown Tkacz
Spokane, Washington

Little Lower than the Angels

Psalm 8 is a much quoted celebration of the peculiar honour accorded humanity as the centrepiece of God's creation, and having 'dominion' (8:6) over it: 'Out of the mouth of babes and sucklings,' he writes, 'hast thou ordained strength... What is man, that thou art mindful of him, and the son of man, that thou visitest him? For thou hast made him a little lower than the angels, and hast crowned him with glory and honour' (8:2, 4–5). For St Augustine the 'babes and sucklings' are those children who responded to Jesus openly (Matthew 21:16) and though young in the faith, having begun 'by belief in the Scriptures... arrive at the knowledge of thy glory' (*Enarrationes in Psalmos*, 8.5–7). The 'son of man' who visits man is 'the very Lord of Man, born of the Virgin Mary' (11); 'a little lower than the angels' is to say just beneath the glory of the heavenly realm. This Psalm is invoked by Chaucer's Prioress in the Prologue to her tale, though only verse 2 is cited. Hamlet's speech to Rosencrantz and Guildenstern responds directly to verses 4–5: 'What a piece of work is man! How noble in reason! How infinite in faculty! In form and moving how express and admirable! In action how like an angel!' (2.2.315–18). Mark Twain applies the hierarchy to humanity's moral sense in his essay 'The Damned Human Race', where in his view 'there is only one possible stage below the Moral Sense: that is the Immoral Sense. The Frenchman has it. Man is but little lower than the angels. This definitely locates him. He is between the angels and the French.'

David L. Jeffrey
University of Ottawa

Miserere, Domine

The opening words of Psalm 51 (Psalm 50, Vulgate) in Latin are *Miserere mei, Deus*; numerous Latin hymns on this theme, as well as both Latin and vernacular settings of the Psalm for liturgical use, are called by one or another form of the 'Have mercy upon me, O Lord' appeal. 'O miserere, Domine' is the refrain of Sir Walter Scott's poem 'The Monks of Bangor's March', and 'Miserere, Domine' is the refrain of Coleridge's 'A Voice Sings'.

David L. Jeffrey
University of Ottawa

Out of the Mouth of Babes

'Out of the mouth of babes and sucklings hast thou ordained strength... that thou mightest still the enemy and the avenger.' The second verse of Psalm 8 associates the strength of God with the innocence of children. The verse has formed part of the liturgy of the Feast of Holy Innocents since as early as the 8th century and has been included in the collect for that feast day in the *Book of Common Prayer* since 1661. The phrase 'out of the mouth of babes' has come to be popularly used of children or of innocents who speak the truth which adults or the more sophisticated either do not see or lack the candour to state. It is often set side by side with Matthew 11:25, where Jesus speaks of spiritual knowledge 'hid... from the wise and prudent' but 'revealed... unto babes'. Although some modern translations of the Bible associate the first part of Psalm 8:2 with the second part of verse 1 (e.g., Revised Standard Version, 'Thou whose glory above the heavens is chanted / by the mouth of babes and infants'; see also Jerusalem Bible), the King James Version and *Book of Common Prayer* retain the Vulgate reading, which is also reflected in the Matthew 21:16 quotation of the Old Testament passage.

The psalm has been versified by numerous English poets, notably Sidney and Milton. Chaucer's Prioress, herself an innocent of sorts, paraphrases verses 1–2 as the opening theme of her tale:

'O Lord, oure Lord, thy name how merveillous
Is in this large world ysprad,' quod she;
'For noght oonly thy laude precious
Parfourned is by men of dignitee,
But by the mouth of children thy bountee

Parfourned is, for on the brest soukynge
Somtyme shewen they thyn heriynge.'

She returns to the phrase later in her tale (*Canterbury Tales*, 7.607–08).

Shakespeare frequently assigns a witty wisdom to children – for example, to Macduff's prattling son in *Macbeth* (4.2) and to the young Prince of York in *Richard III* (3.1). Also his fools, such as Lear's fool and Lavatch in *All's Well*, are childlike adults who voice proverbial wisdom. (In Dostoyevsky's *The Idiot*, Prince Mysteru is likewise a strangely wise innocent.)

Psalm 8:2 fits neatly with Wordsworth's conception of the innocence of children and their closeness to God; he uses the phrase 'babes and sucklings' in the sonnet 'Young England', and the thought may lie behind his various attributions of wisdom or knowledge to children or child-like adults (see, e.g., *Prelude*, 1850, 2.232–55; 13.183; 'Immortality Ode'). Both Byron and Tennyson use the innocence of 'babes and sucklings' ironically. Byron compares the distress of 'ladies who cannot have their own way' with that of animals robbed of their 'babes and sucklings' (*Don Juan*, 5.133), and Tennyson puts the phrase into the mouth of St Thomas Becket, who derives great satisfaction from the praise accorded him by a crowd of people for confronting the secular powers (*Becket*, 2.2.158).

Phillip Rogers
Queen's University, Kingston, Ontario

Rivers of Babylon

Super flumina Babylonis begins the Vulgate version of Psalm 137: 'By the rivers of Babylon we sat down and wept: yea, we wept when we remembered Sion' (King James Version). This lament out of the captivity of Israel, one of the most moving in the Bible, has produced many translations and adaptations. It is still sung by Jews in memory of the captivity, and from the time of the early Church it also became a familiar part of Christian hymnody. St Augustine's sermon on Psalm 137 allegorizes the waters of Babylon as 'all things which here are loved, and pass away' (*Enarrationes in Psalmos*, 137.2).

Izaak Walton relates, in his *Life of Dr John Donne*, how Donne grieved over his wife's death: 'as the Israelites sate mourning by rivers of Babylon when they remembered Sion, so he gave some ease to his oppressed heart by thus venting his sorrow.' Byron has two poems on the subject. In 'By the Rivers of Babylon We Sat Down and Wept', the speaker is one of those who wept, 'and thought of the day / When our foe, in the hue of his slaughterers, / Made Salem's high places his prey.' In 'Oh Weep for Those!' he invites his reader to identify compassionately with 'those that wept by Babel's stream, / Whose shrines are desolate, whose land a dream'. Swinburne's poem celebrating the resistance of Italy to Austrian tyranny, *Super flumina Babylonis*, identifies Italy with captive Israel, 'that for ages of agony has endured, and slept...' Hardy gives voice to his quarrel with the Bible he knows so well when, in *The Return of the Native*, he writes:

> Human beings, in their generous endeavour to construct a hypothesis that shall not degrade a First Cause, have always hesitated to conceive a dominant power of lower moral quality than their own; and, even while they sit down and weep by the waters of Babylon, invent excuses for the oppression which prompts their tears. (6.1)

A similar viewpoint is represented by Ruskin in his *Fors Clavigera* (Letter 91). The narrator of Eliot's *The Waste Land* describes his post-party emptiness with an allusion to the verse, replacing 'Babylon' with 'Leman', a Middle English word for 'lover': 'By the waters of Leman I sat down and wept.' Elizabeth Smart's autobiographical *By Grand Central Station I Sat Down and Wept* recalls the verse in order to lend poignancy to her own often bitter recollections of an alienated and 'exiled' life.

David L. Jeffrey
University of Ottawa

Tale that is Told

Psalm 90, which is called in the rubric of the King James Version 'A Prayer of Moses the man of God', compares the transience and impermanence of sinful human life to the majesty, righteousness, and eternality of God: 'For all our days are passed away in thy wrath: we spend our years as a tale that is told' (90:9; cf. Vulgate *anni nostri sicut aranea meditabuntur*, 'our years shall be considered as a spider' – where the Hebrew has a word meaning 'sigh', St Jerome apparently confused it with the Syriac word for spider, which had in fact already been brought into the Septuagint).

Shakespeare makes frequent allusions to the text, as when Friar Lawrence relates what has happened at the end of *Romeo and Juliet*: 'I will be brief, for my short date of breath / Is not so long as is a tedious tale' (5.3.230–31). In *King John* the melancholy Dauphin of France complains, 'Life is as tedious as a twice-told tale, / Vexing the ear of a drowsy man' (3.4.108–09), and Macbeth, hearing that Lady Macbeth is dead, speaks out of the nihilism which his own life has come to typify:

> Life's but a walking shadow…
> It is a tale
> Told by an idiot, full of sound and fury,
> Signifying nothing. (*Macbeth*, 5.5.24–28)

This rendering provides, in turn, the title of Faulkner's *The Sound and the Fury* as well as Rose Macaulay's *Told by an Idiot*. Washington Irving recalls the biblical passage while touring the monuments in 'Westminster Abbey': 'Thus man passes away; his name perishes from record and recollection; his history is as a tale that is told, and his very monument becomes a ruin.' Because of the prominence accorded Psalm 90 in the liturgy of the *Book of Common Prayer* the verse is frequently quoted in 19th-century reflections on impermanence. In Dickens' *The Old Curiosity Shop*, a homecoming provokes a philosophical observation: 'The old house had long ago been pulled down and a fine broad road was in its place… So do things pass away, like a tale that is told!' (chapter 73). The phrase has ominous portent in Hardy's *Tess of the D'Urbervilles*, where the narrator describes 'the new residents in the garden, taking as much interest in their own doings as if the homestead had never passed its primal time in conjunction with the histories of others, besides which the histories of these were but as a tale that is told' (chapter 54).

David L. Jeffrey
University of Ottawa

Vale of Tears

The Bible conveys such a strong sense of *lachrymae rerum* that St Jerome was able to say that 'the first man... was cast down from paradise into this vale of tears' (Nicene and Post-Nicene Fathers, 6.26). The phrase 'vale of tears,' which is ubiquitous in English literature, derives from the Septuagint translation of Psalm 84:5–6, where the Hebrew phrase 'valley of Baca' was confused with Hebrew *bakah*, 'weeping', and rendered 'valley of weeping', thus entering into Western tradition through the Vulgate translation, '*in valle lacrymarum*' (Psalm 83:7). The idea of earthly existence as a vale of tears owes also to the biblical promise that God's final salvation will include the wiping away of all tears (Isaiah 25:8; Revelation 7:17; 21:4). This same promise is reflected in the beatitude, 'Blessed are ye that weep now: for ye shall laugh' (Luke 6:21; cf. Matthew 5:4).

Weeping in the Scriptures is frequently the external manifestation of penitence (Ezra 10:1; Nehemiah 1:4; Joel 2:12–17; Matthew 26:75; Luke 23:28) and is regarded as a prime evidence of contrition by many exegetes. The tears of repentance are alluded to in Chaucer's *Parson's Tale* (*Canterbury Tales*, 10.993–94) and in *The Tale of Melibee*, though in the latter Prudence commends the patience of Job in distinguishing for the weeper 'attempree weeping' from 'outrageous weeping'. Milton ends book 10 of his *Paradise Lost* with Adam and Eve shedding tears of contrition; when Michael reveals the history of humanity in the following book, they realize that 'the world erelong a world of tears must weep' (11.627), but when they leave Eden their realization of the *felix culpa* wipes away their 'natural tears' (12.645; cf. Revelation 7:17; 21:4). Herbert's 'Altar' is 'Made of a heart and cemented with tears' (2) and, after sin has stained the marble of the 'Church-floore', 'all is cleansed when the marble weeps' (15). Drowning in tears is linked to the flood by Milton (*Patrologia Latina*, 11.754–58) and by Donne ('Holy Sonnet 5'; cf. Lamentations 2:19), who elsewhere makes tears a type of baptism (*Sermons*, 9.290–91). Tears are regarded as God-sends by Cowper in 'To a Protestant Lady' (47–50) and by Blake in 'The Grey Monk', where they are 'intellectual' (i.e., imaginative) things. Elizabeth Barrett Browning's poem 'Tears' is effectively a meditation on the beatitude,

'Blessed are they who mourn, for they shall be comforted.' For Hopkins, tears are a 'melting', a 'madrigal' (*Wreck of the Deutschland*, stanza 18); for Auden, a 'healing fountain' in the 'deserts of the heart' ('In Memory of W.B. Yeats'). Dew is an emblem for tears in Marvell's 'On a Drop of Dew' and in Herrick's 'To Primroses filled with Morning-dew', a poem whose 'lecture' confirms the perception that 'we came crying hither' (Shakespeare, *King Lear*, 4.6.175). The tears in 'Jesus weeping [1],' and elsewhere in Vaughan, are compared to 'soul-quickning rain' (10) and 'live dew' (14). In the Cowper poem, tears find an analogue in the dew on Gideon's fleece (Judges 6:36–40). The bottle of tears connected with the penance of Spenser's Mirabella (*Faerie Queene*, 6.8.24) and mentioned in Herbert's 'Praise [III]' and Vaughan's 'The seed growing secretly' is an image doubly related to Psalm 56:8 and the story of Ishmael (Genesis 21:14–19). The impenitent Ahab in Melville's *Moby Dick* can muster only a single tear, but even it is redeemed by an 'allusive comparison' to the widow's mite of Mark 12:41–44 (see H.T. Walter, *Moby Dick and Calvinism*, 1977, 148).

Perhaps the most compelling of Old Testament treatments of tears is Psalm 137, which begins 'By the rivers of Babylon, there we sat down, yea, we wept, when we remembered Zion.' Versions of this psalm were written not only by authors such as the Countess of Pembroke, Campion, Bacon, Crashaw, Carew, and Denham, but also by Byron, Swinburne, and C. Rossetti. Burns puts it to humorous use in 'The Ordination', and T.S. Eliot refers to it ironically in *The Waste Land* (182), where tears become part of the poem's water imagery.

Ronald B. Bond
University of Calgary

Valley of the Shadow of Death

There are many Old Testament instances of the phrase 'shadow of death' in the King James Version (e.g., Job 3:5; 10:21, 22; 24:17; 34:22; 38:17; Amos 5:8; Jeremiah 2:6; 13:16), but the most influential uses of the phrase are in Psalm 107:10, Isaiah 9:2, and, of course, Psalm 23:4, with its 'valley of the shadow of death'.

Marginal notes to the Geneva Bible refer to one who is 'in

danger of death as ye shepe that wandreth in the darke valley without his shepherd' – perhaps providing a hint for Bunyan's most famous use of the image. Of Bunyan's Valley of the Shadow in part 2 of *Pilgrim's Progress*, certain travellers who have abandoned their pilgrimage report that

> the Valley it self... is as dark as pitch: we also saw there Hobgoblins, Satyrs, and Dragons of the Pit: We heard also in that Valley a continual howling and yelling, as of a People under unutterable misery; who there sat bound in affliction and Irons: and over that Valley hangs the discouraging cloud of confusion, death also doth always spread his wings over it: in a word, it is every wit dreadful, being utterly without Order.

Christian, hearing of such horrors, prudently puts up his sword and turns to 'All-Prayer'. The moral drawn from Job 12:22 stresses in paradoxical terms the victory of Providence over the threat posed by the Valley of the Shadow: 'He discovereth deep things out of darkness, and bringeth out to light the shadow of death.'

Notable among other literary allusions is the recollection of Chaucer's Parson (*Canterbury Tales*, 10.177) of Job's apprehension of the afterlife – 'the lond of mysese and of derknesse, where as is the shadwe of deeth, where as ther is noon ordre or ordinaunce, but grisly drede that evere shal laste.' The dying Bosola in Webster's *Duchess of Malfi*, thinking rather of life as a kind of living hell, adds a level of angst (and misogyny) to the reference: 'O, this gloomy world! / In what a shadow, or deep pit of darkness, / Doth womanish and fearful mankind live!'

The valley of the shadow has an important place in Poe's *Eldorado*, an evocative poem about the universality of death. And Shaw's Major Barbara, abandoning her Salvationist creed, pronounces a secularized version of Bunyan's paradoxes: the way to life, she says, lies 'through the raising of hell to heaven and of man to God, through the unveiling of the eternal light in the Valley of the Shadow'.

Richard Schell
Laurentian University

THE PSALMS

Part One

Hymns of Praise

THE EXCELLENCE OF GOD
Psalm 8

O Lord our Lord,
  how excellent is thy name in all the earth!
who hast set thy glory
  above the heavens.

Out of the mouth of babes and sucklings
  hast thou ordained strength
because of thine enemies,
  that thou mightest still the enemy and the avenger.

When I consider thy heavens,
  the work of thy fingers,
the moon and the stars,
  which thou hast ordained;
What is man, that thou art mindful of him?
  and the son of man, that thou visitest him?
For thou hast made him a little lower than the angels,
  and hast crowned him with glory and honour.

Thou madest him to have dominion over the works of
    thy hands;
  thou hast put all things under his feet:
All sheep and oxen,
  yea, and the beasts of the field;
The fowl of the air,
  and the fish of the sea,
  and whatsoever passeth through the paths of the seas.

O Lord our Lord,
  how excellent is thy name in all the earth!

THE GLORY OF GOD
Psalm 19

The heavens declare the glory of God;
    and the firmament sheweth his handywork.
Day unto day uttereth speech,
    and night unto night sheweth knowledge.
There is no speech nor language,
    where their voice is not heard.
Their line is gone out through all the earth,
    and their words to the end of the world.

In them hath he set a tabernacle for the sun,
    which is as a bridegroom coming out of his chamber,
    and rejoiceth as a strong man to run a race.
His going forth is from the end of the heaven,
    and his circuit unto the ends of it:
    and there is nothing hid from the heat thereof.

The law of the Lord is perfect, converting the soul:
    the testimony of the Lord is sure, making wise the simple.
The statutes of the Lord are right, rejoicing the heart:
    the commandment of the Lord is pure, enlightening
        the eyes.
The fear of the Lord is clean, enduring for ever:
    the judgments of the Lord are true and righteous altogether.
More to be desired are they than gold, yea, than much
        fine gold:
    sweeter also than honey and the honeycomb.
Moreover by them is thy servant warned:
    and in keeping of them there is great reward.

Who can understand his errors?
    cleanse thou me from secret faults.
Keep back thy servant also from presumptuous sins;
    let them not have dominion over me:
then shall I be upright,
    and I shall be innocent from the great transgression.

Let the words of my mouth, and the meditation of my heart,
    be acceptable in thy sight,
    O Lord, my strength, and my redeemer.

THE GOODNESS OF GOD
Psalm 33

Rejoice in the Lord, O ye righteous:
    for praise is comely for the upright.
Praise the Lord with harp:
    sing unto him with the psaltery and an instrument
        of ten strings.
Sing unto him a new song;
    play skilfully with a loud noise.

For the word of the Lord is right; and all his works
        are done in truth.
He loveth righteousness and judgment:
    the earth is full of the goodness of the Lord.

By the word of the Lord were the heavens made;
    and all the host of them by the breath of his mouth.
He gathereth the waters of the sea together as an heap:
    he layeth up the depth in storehouses.
Let all the earth fear the Lord:
    let all the inhabitants of the world stand in awe of him.
For he spake, and it was done;
    he commanded, and it stood fast.
The Lord bringeth the counsel of the heathen to nought:
    he maketh the devices of the people of none effect.
The counsel of the Lord standeth for ever,
    the thoughts of his heart to all generations.

Blessed is the nation whose God is the Lord;
    and the people whom he hath chosen for his own inheritance.
The Lord looketh from heaven;
    he beholdeth all the sons of men.

From the place of his habitation he looketh upon
    all the inhabitants of the earth.
He fashioneth their hearts alike;
    he considereth all their works.
There is no king saved by the multitude of an host:
    a mighty man is not delivered by much strength.
An horse is a vain thing for safety:
    neither shall he deliver any by his great strength.
Behold, the eye of the Lord is upon them that fear him,
    upon them that hope in his mercy;
to deliver their soul from death,
    and to keep them alive in famine.

Our soul waiteth for the Lord:
    he is our help and our shield.
For our heart shall rejoice in him,
    because we have trusted in his holy name.
Let thy mercy, O Lord, be upon us,
    according as we hope in thee.

AN INVITATION TO PRAISE
Psalm 100

Make a joyful noise unto the Lord, all ye lands.
    Serve the Lord with gladness:
    come before his presence with singing.
Know ye that the Lord he is God:
    it is he that hath made us, and not we ourselves;
    we are his people, and the sheep of his pasture.

Enter into his gates with thanksgiving,
    and into his courts with praise:
    be thankful unto him, and bless his name.
For the Lord is good; his mercy is everlasting;
    and his truth endureth to all generations.

THE GOD OF LOVE
Psalm 103

Bless the Lord, O my soul:
    and all that is within me, bless his holy name.
Bless the Lord, O my soul,
    and forget not all his benefits:
who forgiveth all thine iniquities;
    who healeth all thy diseases;
who redeemeth thy life from destruction;
    who crowneth thee with lovingkindness and tender
      mercies;
who satisfieth thy mouth with good things;
    so that thy youth is renewed like the eagle's.

The Lord executeth righteousness
    and judgment for all that are oppressed.

He made known his ways unto Moses,
    his acts unto the children of Israel.
The Lord is merciful and gracious,
    slow to anger, and plenteous in mercy.
He will not always chide:
    neither will he keep his anger for ever.
He hath not dealt with us after our sins;
    nor rewarded us according to our iniquities.
For as the heaven is high above the earth,
    so great is his mercy toward them that fear him.
As far as the east is from the west,
    so far hath he removed our transgressions from us.
Like as a father pitieth his children,
    so the Lord pitieth them that fear him.
For he knoweth our frame;
    he remembereth that we are dust.
As for man, his days are as grass:
    as a flower of the field, so he flourisheth.
For the wind passeth over it, and it is gone;
    and the place thereof shall know it no more.

But the mercy of the Lord is from everlasting to everlasting
upon them that fear him,
and his righteousness unto children's children;
To such as keep his covenant,
and to those that remember his commandments to do them.

The Lord hath prepared his throne in the heavens;
and his kingdom ruleth over all.

Bless the Lord, ye his angels,
that excel in strength, that do his commandments,
hearkening unto the voice of his word.
Bless ye the Lord, all ye his hosts;
ye ministers of his, that do his pleasure.
Bless the Lord, all his works in all places of his dominion:
bless the Lord, O my soul.

THE GOD OF CREATION
Psalm 104

Bless the Lord, O my soul.

O Lord my God, thou art very great;
thou art clothed with honour and majesty.
Who coverest thyself with light as with a garment:
who stretchest out the heavens like a curtain:
who layeth the beams of his chambers in the waters:
who maketh the clouds his chariot:
who walketh upon the wings of the wind:
who maketh his angels spirits;
his ministers a flaming fire:
who laid the foundations of the earth,
that it should not be removed for ever.
Thou coveredst it with the deep as with a garment:
the waters stood above the mountains.
At thy rebuke they fled;
at the voice of thy thunder they hasted away.

They go up by the mountains;
    they go down by the valleys
      unto the place which thou hast founded for them.
Thou hast set a bound that they may not pass over;
    that they turn not again to cover the earth.

He sendeth the springs into the valleys,
    which run among the hills.
They give drink to every beast of the field:
    the wild asses quench their thirst.
By them shall the fowls of the heaven have their habitation,
    which sing among the branches.
He watereth the hills from his chambers:
    the earth is satisfied with the fruit of thy works.
He causeth the grass to grow for the cattle,
    and herb for the service of man:
      that he may bring forth food out of the earth;
and wine that maketh glad the heart of man,
    and oil to make his face to shine,
      and bread which strengtheneth man's heart.
The trees of the Lord are full of sap;
    the cedars of Lebanon, which he hath planted;
where the birds make their nests:
    as for the stork, the fir trees are her house.
The high hills are a refuge for the wild goats;
    and the rocks for the conies.

He appointed the moon for seasons:
    the sun knoweth his going down.
Thou makest darkness, and it is night:
    wherein all the beasts of the forest do creep forth.
The young lions roar after their prey,
    and seek their meat from God.
The sun ariseth, they gather themselves together,
    and lay them down in their dens.
Man goeth forth unto his work
    and to his labour until the evening.

O Lord, how manifold are thy works!
    in wisdom hast thou made them all:
    the earth is full of thy riches.
So is this great and wide sea,
    wherein are things creeping innumerable,
    both small and great beasts.
There go the ships:
    there is that leviathan, whom thou hast made to play therein.

These wait all upon thee;
    that thou mayest give them their meat in due season.
That thou givest them they gather:
    thou openest thine hand, they are filled with good.
Thou hidest thy face, they are troubled:
    thou takest away their breath, they die, and return to
       their dust.
Thou sendest forth thy spirit,
    they are created:
    and thou renewest the face of the earth.

The glory of the Lord shall endure for ever:
    the Lord shall rejoice in his works.
He looketh on the earth, and it trembleth:
    he toucheth the hills, and they smoke.
I will sing unto the Lord as long as I live:
    I will sing praise to my God while I have my being.
My meditation of him shall be sweet:
    I will be glad in the Lord.
Let the sinners be consumed out of the earth,
    and let the wicked be no more.

Bless thou the Lord, O my soul.

Praise ye the Lord.

THE GOD OF ALL NATIONS
Psalm 117

O praise the Lord, all ye nations:
  praise him, all ye people.
For his merciful kindness is great toward us:
  and the truth of the Lord endureth for ever.

Praise ye the Lord.

THE MAJESTY OF GOD
Psalm 145

I will extol thee, my God, O king;
  and I will bless thy name for ever and ever.
Every day will I bless thee;
  and I will praise thy name for ever and ever.

Great is the Lord, and greatly to be praised;
  and his greatness is unsearchable.
One generation shall praise thy works to another,
  and shall declare thy mighty acts.
I will speak of the glorious honour of thy majesty,
  and of thy wondrous works.
And men shall speak of the might of thy terrible acts:
  and I will declare thy greatness.
They shall abundantly utter the memory of thy great
    goodness,
  and shall sing of thy righteousness.
The Lord is gracious, and full of compassion;
  slow to anger, and of great mercy.
The Lord is good to all:
  and his tender mercies are over all his works.
All thy works shall praise thee, O Lord;
  and thy saints shall bless thee.

They shall speak of the glory of thy kingdom,
    and talk of thy power;
to make known to the sons of men his mighty acts,
    and the glorious majesty of his kingdom.
Thy kingdom is an everlasting kingdom,
    and thy dominion endureth throughout all generations.

The Lord upholdeth all that fall,
    and raiseth up all those that be bowed down.
The eyes of all wait upon thee;
    and thou givest them their meat in due season.
Thou openest thine hand,
    and satisfiest the desire of every living thing.

The Lord is righteous in all his ways,
    and holy in all his works.
The Lord is nigh unto all them that call upon him,
    to all that call upon him in truth.
He will fulfil the desire of them that fear him:
    he also will hear their cry, and will save them.
The Lord preserveth all them that love him:
    but all the wicked will he destroy.

My mouth shall speak the praise of the Lord:
    and let all flesh bless his holy name
    for ever and ever.

THE COMPASSION OF GOD
Psalm 146

Praise ye the Lord.

Praise the Lord, O my soul.
    While I live will I praise the Lord:
    I will sing praises unto my God while I have any being.

Put not your trust in princes,
    nor in the son of man, in whom there is no help.

His breath goeth forth, he returneth to his earth;
    in that very day his thoughts perish.

Happy is he that hath the God of Jacob for his help,
    whose hope is in the Lord his God:
which made heaven, and earth,
    the sea, and all that therein is:
    which keepeth truth for ever:
which executeth judgment for the oppressed:
    which giveth food to the hungry.
The Lord looseth the prisoners:
    the Lord openeth the eyes of the blind:
the Lord raiseth them that are bowed down:
    the Lord loveth the righteous:
the Lord preserveth the strangers;
    he relieveth the fatherless and widow:
    but the way of the wicked he turneth upside down.

The Lord shall reign for ever,
    even thy God, O Zion, unto all generations.

Praise ye the Lord.

THE POWER OF GOD'S WORD
Psalm 147

Praise ye the Lord:
    for it is good to sing praises unto our God;
    for it is pleasant; and praise is comely.

The Lord doth build up Jerusalem:
    he gathereth together the outcasts of Israel.
He healeth the broken in heart,
    and bindeth up their wounds.

He telleth the number of the stars;
    he calleth them all by their names.

Great is our Lord, and of great power:
>   his understanding is infinite.
The Lord lifteth up the meek:
>   he casteth the wicked down to the ground.

Sing unto the Lord with thanksgiving;
>   sing praise upon the harp unto our God:
Who covereth the heaven with clouds,
>   who prepareth rain for the earth,
>   who maketh grass to grow upon the mountains.
He giveth to the beast his food,
>   and to the young ravens which cry.

He delighteth not in the strength of the horse:
>   he taketh not pleasure in the legs of a man.
The Lord taketh pleasure in them that fear him,
>   in those that hope in his mercy.

Praise the Lord, O Jerusalem;
>   praise thy God, O Zion.
For he hath strengthened the bars of thy gates;
>   he hath blessed thy children within thee.
He maketh peace in thy borders,
>   and filleth thee with the finest of the wheat.

He sendeth forth his commandment upon earth:
>   his word runneth very swiftly.
He giveth snow like wool:
>   he scattereth the hoarfrost like ashes.
He casteth forth his ice like morsels:
>   who can stand before his cold?
He sendeth out his word, and melteth them:
>   he causeth his wind to blow, and the waters flow.
He sheweth his word unto Jacob,
>   his statutes and his judgments unto Israel.
He hath not dealt so with any nation:
>   and as for his judgments, they have not known them.

Praise ye the Lord.

THE PRAISE OF CREATION
Psalm 148

Praise ye the Lord.

Praise ye the Lord from the heavens:
   praise him in the heights.
Praise ye him, all his angels:
   praise ye him, all his hosts.
Praise ye him, sun and moon:
   praise him, all ye stars of light.
Praise him, ye heavens of heavens,
   and ye waters that be above the heavens.
Let them praise the name of the Lord:
   for he commanded, and they were created.
He hath also stablished them for ever and ever:
   he hath made a decree which shall not pass.

Praise the Lord from the earth,
   ye dragons, and all deeps:
fire, and hail; snow, and vapour;
   stormy wind fulfilling his word:
mountains, and all hills;
   fruitful trees, and all cedars:
beasts, and all cattle;
   creeping things, and flying fowl:
kings of the earth, and all people;
   princes, and all judges of the earth:
both young men, and maidens;
   old men, and children:
let them praise the name of the Lord:
   for his name alone is excellent;
   his glory is above the earth and heaven.
He also exalteth the horn of his people,
   the praise of all his saints;
   even of the children of Israel, a people near unto him.

Praise ye the Lord.

PRAISE GOD IN MUSIC AND SONG
Psalm 150

Praise ye the Lord.

Praise God in his sanctuary:
    praise him in the firmament of his power.
Praise him for his mighty acts:
    praise him according to his excellent greatness.
Praise him with the sound of the trumpet:
    praise him with the psaltery and harp.
Praise him with the timbrel and dance:
    praise him with stringed instruments and organs.
Praise him upon the loud cymbals:
    praise him upon the high sounding cymbals.

Let every thing that hath breath praise the Lord.

Praise ye the Lord.

Part Two

Hymns of Trust

CONFIDENCE IN GOD
Psalm 11

In the Lord put I my trust:
    how say ye to my soul,
    Flee as a bird to your mountain?
For, lo, the wicked bend their bow,
    they make ready their arrow upon the string,
    that they may privily shoot at the upright in heart.
If the foundations be destroyed,
    what can the righteous do?

The Lord is in his holy temple,
    the Lord's throne is in heaven:
his eyes behold, his eyelids try,
    the children of men.
The Lord trieth the righteous:
    but the wicked and him that loveth violence
    his soul hateth.
Upon the wicked he shall rain
    snares, fire and brimstone, and an horrible tempest:
    this shall be the portion of their cup.

For the righteous Lord loveth righteousness;
    his countenance doth behold the upright.

JOY IN GOD'S PRESENCE
Psalm 16

Preserve me, O God:
 for in thee do I put my trust.

O my soul, thou hast said unto the Lord, Thou art my Lord:
 my goodness extendeth not to thee;
but to the saints that are in the earth,
 and to the excellent, in whom is all my delight.
Their sorrows shall be multiplied
 that hasten after another god:
their drink offerings of blood will I not offer,
 nor take up their names into my lips.

The Lord is the portion of mine inheritance and of my cup:
 thou maintainest my lot.
The lines are fallen unto me in pleasant places;
 yea, I have a goodly heritage.

I will bless the Lord, who hath given me counsel:
 my reins also instruct me in the night seasons.
I have set the Lord always before me:
 because he is at my right hand,
 I shall not be moved.

Therefore my heart is glad, and my glory rejoiceth:
 my flesh also shall rest in hope.
For thou wilt not leave my soul in hell;
 neither wilt thou suffer thine Holy One to see corruption.
Thou wilt shew me the path of life:
 in thy presence is fulness of joy;
 at thy right hand there are pleasures for evermore.

THE SHEPHERD PSALM
Psalm 23

The Lord is my shepherd; I shall not want.
He maketh me to lie down in green pastures:
    he leadeth me beside the still waters.
He restoreth my soul:
    he leadeth me in the paths of righteousness for his
        name's sake.
Yea, though I walk
    through the valley of the shadow of death,
I will fear no evil:
    for thou art with me;
thy rod and thy staff
    they comfort me.

Thou preparest a table before me
    in the presence of mine enemies:
thou anointest my head with oil;
    my cup runneth over.
Surely goodness and mercy shall follow me
    all the days of my life:
and I will dwell in the house of the Lord for ever.

A DECLARATION OF FAITH
Psalm 27

The Lord is my light and my salvation;
    whom shall I fear?
the Lord is the strength of my life;
    of whom shall I be afraid?
When the wicked, even mine enemies and my foes,
    came upon me to eat up my flesh, they stumbled and fell.
Though an host should encamp against me,
    my heart shall not fear:
though war should rise against me,
    in this will I be confident.

One thing have I desired of the Lord,
    that will I seek after;
that I may dwell in the house of the Lord
    all the days of my life,
to behold the beauty of the Lord,
    and to enquire in his temple.
For in the time of trouble
    he shall hide me in his pavilion:
in the secret of his tabernacle shall he hide me;
    he shall set me up upon a rock.
And now shall mine head be lifted up
    above mine enemies round about me:
therefore will I offer in his tabernacle sacrifices of joy;
    I will sing, yea, I will sing praises unto the Lord.

Hear, O Lord, when I cry with my voice:
    have mercy also upon me, and answer me.
When thou saidst, Seek ye my face;
    my heart said unto thee, Thy face, Lord, will I seek.
Hide not thy face far from me;
    put not thy servant away in anger:
    thou hast been my help;
leave me not, neither forsake me,
    O God of my salvation.
When my father and my mother forsake me,
    then the Lord will take me up.
Teach me thy way, O Lord,
    and lead me in a plain path,
    because of mine enemies.
Deliver me not over unto the will of mine enemies:
    for false witnesses are risen up against me,
    and such as breathe out cruelty.

I had fainted, unless I had believed
    to see the goodness of the Lord
    in the land of the living.
Wait on the Lord:
    be of good courage, and he shall strengthen thine heart:
    wait, I say, on the Lord.

A DESIRE FOR GOD
Psalm 63

O God, thou art my God;
   early will I seek thee:
my soul thirsteth for thee,
   my flesh longeth for thee
in a dry and thirsty land,
   where no water is;

To see thy power and thy glory,
   so as I have seen thee in the sanctuary.
Because thy lovingkindness is better than life,
   my lips shall praise thee.
Thus will I bless thee while I live:
   I will lift up my hands in thy name.
My soul shall be satisfied as with marrow and fatness;
   and my mouth shall praise thee with joyful lips:
when I remember thee upon my bed,
   and meditate on thee in the night watches.

Because thou hast been my help,
   therefore in the shadow of thy wings will I rejoice.
My soul followeth hard after thee:
   thy right hand upholdeth me.

But those that seek my soul, to destroy it,
   shall go into the lower parts of the earth.
They shall fall by the sword:
   they shall be a portion for foxes.

But the king shall rejoice in God;
   every one that sweareth by him shall glory:
   but the mouth of them that speak lies shall be stopped.

GOD WILL PROTECT
Psalm 91

He that dwelleth in the secret place of the most High
   shall abide under the shadow of the Almighty.
I will say of the Lord, He is my refuge and my fortress:
   my God; in him will I trust.

Surely he shall deliver thee from the snare of the fowler,
   and from the noisome pestilence.
He shall cover thee with his feathers,
   and under his wings shalt thou trust:
   his truth shall be thy shield and buckler.
Thou shalt not be afraid for the terror by night;
   nor for the arrow that flieth by day;
Nor for the pestilence that walketh in darkness;
   nor for the destruction that wasteth at noonday.
A thousand shall fall at thy side,
   and ten thousand at thy right hand;
   but it shall not come nigh thee.
Only with thine eyes shalt thou behold
   and see the reward of the wicked.

Because thou hast made the Lord, which is my refuge,
   even the most High, thy habitation;
there shall no evil befall thee,
   neither shall any plague come nigh thy dwelling.
For he shall give his angels charge over thee,
   to keep thee in all thy ways.
They shall bear thee up in their hands,
   lest thou dash thy foot against a stone.
Thou shalt tread upon the lion and adder:
   the young lion and the dragon shalt thou trample
      under feet.

Because he hath set his love upon me, therefore will I
    deliver him:
  I will set him on high, because he hath known my name.
He shall call upon me, and I will answer him:
  I will be with him in trouble;
  I will deliver him, and honour him.
With long life will I satisfy him,
    and shew him my salvation.

GOD WILL PRESERVE
Psalm 121

I will lift up mine eyes unto the hills,
  from whence cometh my help.
My help cometh from the Lord,
  which made heaven and earth.

He will not suffer thy foot to be moved:
  he that keepeth thee will not slumber.
Behold, he that keepeth Israel
  shall neither slumber nor sleep.

The Lord is thy keeper:
  the Lord is thy shade upon thy right hand.
The sun shall not smite thee by day,
  nor the moon by night.

The Lord shall preserve thee from all evil:
  he shall preserve thy soul.
The Lord shall preserve thy going out and thy coming in
  from this time forth, and even for evermore.

A CHILDLIKE TRUST
Psalm 131

Lord, my heart is not haughty,
    nor mine eyes lofty:
neither do I exercise myself in great matters,
    or in things too high for me.
Surely I have behaved and quieted myself,
    as a child that is weaned of his mother:
    my soul is even as a weaned child.

Let Israel hope in the Lord
    from henceforth and for ever.

Part Three

Hymns of Thanksgiving

WEEPING TURNED TO JOY
Psalm 30

I will extol thee, O Lord;
    for thou hast lifted me up,
    and hast not made my foes to rejoice over me.
O Lord my God, I cried unto thee,
    and thou hast healed me.
O Lord, thou hast brought up my soul from the grave:
    thou hast kept me alive, that I should not go down to
        the pit.

Sing unto the Lord, O ye saints of his,
    and give thanks at the remembrance of his holiness.
For his anger endureth but a moment;
    in his favour is life:
weeping may endure for a night,
    but joy cometh in the morning.

And in my prosperity I said,
    I shall never be moved.
Lord, by thy favour thou hast made my mountain to stand
      strong:
    thou didst hide thy face, and I was troubled.

I cried to thee, O Lord;
    and unto the Lord I made supplication.
What profit is there in my blood,
    when I go down to the pit?
Shall the dust praise thee?
    shall it declare thy truth?

Hear, O Lord, and have mercy upon me:
   Lord, be thou my helper.

Thou hast turned for me my mourning into dancing:
   thou hast put off my sackcloth, and girded me with
      gladness;
To the end that my glory may sing praise to thee, and not
    be silent.
   O Lord my God, I will give thanks unto thee for ever.

CONFESSION BRINGS FORGIVENESS
Psalm 32

Blessed is he
   whose transgression is forgiven,
   whose sin is covered.
Blessed is the man
   unto whom the Lord imputeth not iniquity,
   and in whose spirit there is no guile.

When I kept silence,
   my bones waxed old
   through my roaring all the day long.
For day and night
   thy hand was heavy upon me:
my moisture is turned
   into the drought of summer.
I acknowledged my sin unto thee,
   and mine iniquity have I not hid.
I said, I will confess my transgressions unto the Lord;
   and thou forgavest the iniquity of my sin.

For this shall every one that is godly pray unto thee
   in a time when thou mayest be found:
surely in the floods of great waters
   they shall not come nigh unto him.

Thou art my hiding place;
    thou shalt preserve me from trouble;
    thou shalt compass me about with songs of deliverance.

I will instruct thee and teach thee in the way which thou shalt go:
    I will guide thee with mine eye.
Be ye not as the horse, or as the mule,
    which have no understanding:
whose mouth must be held in with bit and bridle,
    lest they come near unto thee.
Many sorrows shall be to the wicked:
    but he that trusteth in the Lord,
    mercy shall compass him about.

Be glad in the Lord, and rejoice, ye righteous:
    and shout for joy, all ye that are upright in heart.

GOD WILL SAVE THE RIGHTEOUS
Psalm 34

I will bless the Lord at all times:
    his praise shall continually be in my mouth.
My soul shall make her boast in the Lord:
    the humble shall hear thereof, and be glad.
O magnify the Lord with me,
    and let us exalt his name together.

I sought the Lord, and he heard me,
    and delivered me from all my fears.
They looked unto him, and were lightened:
    and their faces were not ashamed.
This poor man cried, and the Lord heard him,
    and saved him out of all his troubles.
The angel of the Lord encampeth round about them that
      fear him,
    and delivereth them.

O taste and see that the Lord is good:
   blessed is the man that trusteth in him.
O fear the Lord, ye his saints:
   for there is no want to them that fear him.
The young lions do lack, and suffer hunger:
   but they that seek the Lord shall not want any good thing.

Come, ye children, hearken unto me:
   I will teach you the fear of the Lord.
What man is he that desireth life,
   and loveth many days, that he may see good?
Keep thy tongue from evil,
   and thy lips from speaking guile.
Depart from evil, and do good;
   seek peace, and pursue it.

The eyes of the Lord are upon the righteous,
   and his ears are open unto their cry.
The face of the Lord is against them that do evil,
   to cut off the remembrance of them from the earth.

The righteous cry, and the Lord heareth,
   and delivereth them out of all their troubles.
The Lord is nigh unto them that are of a broken heart;
   and saveth such as be of a contrite spirit.

Many are the afflictions of the righteous:
   but the Lord delivereth him out of them all.
He keepeth all his bones:
   not one of them is broken.

Evil shall slay the wicked:
   and they that hate the righteous shall be desolate.
The Lord redeemeth the soul of his servants:
   and none of them that trust in him shall be desolate.

GOD WITHIN MY HEART
Psalm 40

I waited patiently for the Lord;
 and he inclined unto me, and heard my cry.
He brought me up also out of an horrible pit,
 out of the miry clay,
and set my feet upon a rock,
 and established my goings.
And he hath put a new song in my mouth,
 even praise unto our God:
many shall see it, and fear,
 and shall trust in the Lord.

Blessed is that man
 that maketh the Lord his trust,
and respecteth not the proud,
 nor such as turn aside to lies.
Many, O Lord my God,
 are thy wonderful works which thou hast done,
and thy thoughts which are to us-ward:
 they cannot be reckoned up in order unto thee:
if I would declare and speak of them,
 they are more than can be numbered.

Sacrifice and offering thou didst not desire;
 mine ears hast thou opened:
burnt offering and sin offering
 hast thou not required.
Then said I, Lo, I come:
 in the volume of the book it is written of me,
I delight to do thy will, O my God:
 yea, thy law is within my heart.

I have preached righteousness in the great congregation:
 lo, I have not refrained my lips,
 O Lord, thou knowest.

I have not hid thy righteousness within my heart;
    I have declared thy faithfulness and thy salvation:
I have not concealed thy lovingkindness and thy truth
    from the great congregation.

Withhold not thou thy tender mercies from me, O Lord:
    let thy lovingkindness and thy truth continually preserve me.
For innumerable evils have compassed me about:
    mine iniquities have taken hold upon me,
    so that I am not able to look up;
they are more than the hairs of mine head:
    therefore my heart faileth me.

Be pleased, O Lord, to deliver me:
    O Lord, make haste to help me.
Let them be ashamed and confounded together
    that seek after my soul to destroy it;
let them be driven backward
    and put to shame that wish me evil.
Let them be desolate for a reward of their shame
    that say unto me, Aha, aha.
Let all those that seek thee rejoice and be glad in thee:
    let such as love thy salvation say continually,
    The Lord be magnified.

But I am poor and needy;
    yet the Lord thinketh upon me:
thou art my help and my deliverer;
    make no tarrying, O my God.

GOD'S PROVIDENCE
Psalm 65

Praise waiteth for thee, O God, in Sion:
    and unto thee shall the vow be performed.
O thou that hearest prayer,
    unto thee shall all flesh come.

Iniquities prevail against me:
    as for our transgressions, thou shalt purge them away.
Blessed is the man whom thou choosest,
    and causest to approach unto thee,
    that he may dwell in thy courts:
we shall be satisfied with the goodness of thy house,
    even of thy holy temple.

By terrible things in righteousness wilt thou answer us,
    O God of our salvation;
who art the confidence of all the ends of the earth,
    and of them that are afar off upon the sea:
which by his strength setteth fast the mountains;
    being girded with power:
which stilleth the noise of the seas,
    the noise of their waves,
    and the tumult of the people.
They also that dwell in the uttermost parts
    are afraid at thy tokens:
    thou makest the outgoings of the morning and evening
        to rejoice.

Thou visitest the earth, and waterest it:
    thou greatly enrichest it with the river of God,
    which is full of water:
thou preparest them corn,
    when thou hast so provided for it.
Thou waterest the ridges thereof abundantly:
    thou settlest the furrows thereof:
thou makest it soft with showers:
    thou blessest the springing thereof.
Thou crownest the year with thy goodness;
    and thy paths drop fatness.
They drop upon the pastures of the wilderness:
    and the little hills rejoice on every side.
The pastures are clothed with flocks;
    the valleys also are covered over with corn;
    they shout for joy, they also sing.

GOD'S FAITHFULNESS
Psalm 92

It is a good thing to give thanks unto the Lord,
    and to sing praises unto thy name, O most High:
to shew forth thy lovingkindness in the morning,
    and thy faithfulness every night,
upon an instrument of ten strings, and upon the psaltery;
    upon the harp with a solemn sound.

For thou, Lord, hast made me glad through thy work:
    I will triumph in the works of thy hands.
O Lord, how great are thy works!
    and thy thoughts are very deep.
A brutish man knoweth not;
    neither doth a fool understand this.
When the wicked spring as the grass,
    and when all the workers of iniquity do flourish;
it is that they shall be destroyed for ever:
    but thou, Lord, art most high for evermore.

For, lo, thine enemies, O Lord,
    for, lo, thine enemies shall perish;
    all the workers of iniquity shall be scattered.
But my horn shalt thou exalt like the horn of an unicorn:
    I shall be anointed with fresh oil.
Mine eye also shall see my desire on mine enemies,
    and mine ears shall hear my desire of the wicked
    that rise up against me.

The righteous shall flourish like the palm tree:
    he shall grow like a cedar in Lebanon.
Those that be planted in the house of the Lord
    shall flourish in the courts of our God.
They shall still bring forth fruit in old age;
    they shall be fat and flourishing;
to shew that the Lord is upright:
    he is my rock, and there is no unrighteousness in him.

GOD'S WONDERFUL WORKS
Psalm 107

O give thanks unto the Lord, for he is good:
    for his mercy endureth for ever.
Let the redeemed of the Lord say so,
    whom he hath redeemed from the hand of the enemy;
and gathered them out of the lands,
    from the east, and from the west,
    from the north, and from the south.

They wandered in the wilderness in a solitary way;
    they found no city to dwell in.
Hungry and thirsty,
    their soul fainted in them.
Then they cried unto the Lord in their trouble,
    and he delivered them out of their distresses.
And he led them forth by the right way,
    that they might go to a city of habitation.
Oh that men would praise the Lord for his goodness,
    and for his wonderful works to the children of men!
For he satisfieth the longing soul,
    and filleth the hungry soul with goodness.

Such as sit in darkness and in the shadow of death,
    being bound in affliction and iron;
Because they rebelled against the words of God,
    and contemned the counsel of the most High:
therefore he brought down their heart with labour;
    they fell down, and there was none to help.
Then they cried unto the Lord in their trouble,
    and he saved them out of their distresses.
He brought them out of darkness and the shadow of death,
    and brake their bands in sunder.
Oh that men would praise the Lord for his goodness,
    and for his wonderful works to the children of men!
For he hath broken the gates of brass,
    and cut the bars of iron in sunder.

Fools because of their transgression,
    and because of their iniquities, are afflicted.
Their soul abhorreth all manner of meat;
    and they draw near unto the gates of death.
Then they cry unto the Lord in their trouble,
    and he saveth them out of their distresses.
He sent his word, and healed them,
    and delivered them from their destructions.
Oh that men would praise the Lord for his goodness,
    and for his wonderful works to the children of men!
And let them sacrifice the sacrifices of thanksgiving,
    and declare his works with rejoicing.

They that go down to the sea in ships,
    that do business in great waters;
these see the works of the Lord,
    and his wonders in the deep.
For he commandeth, and raiseth the stormy wind,
    which lifteth up the waves thereof.
They mount up to the heaven, they go down again to
        the depths:
    their soul is melted because of trouble.
They reel to and fro, and stagger like a drunken man,
    and are at their wits' end.
Then they cry unto the Lord in their trouble,
    and he bringeth them out of their distresses.
He maketh the storm a calm,
    so that the waves thereof are still.
Then are they glad because they be quiet;
    so he bringeth them unto their desired haven.
Oh that men would praise the Lord for his goodness,
    and for his wonderful works to the children of men!
Let them exalt him also in the congregation of the people,
    and praise him in the assembly of the elders.

He turneth rivers into a wilderness,
    and the watersprings into dry ground;

a fruitful land into barrenness,
>for the wickedness of them that dwell therein.
He turneth the wilderness into a standing water,
>and dry ground into watersprings.
And there he maketh the hungry to dwell,
>that they may prepare a city for habitation;
and sow the fields, and plant vineyards,
>which may yield fruits of increase.
He blesseth them also, so that they are multiplied greatly;
>and suffereth not their cattle to decrease.

Again, they are minished and brought low
>through oppression, affliction, and sorrow.
He poureth contempt upon princes,
>and causeth them to wander in the wilderness, where
>>there is no way.
Yet setteth he the poor on high from affliction,
>and maketh him families like a flock.
The righteous shall see it, and rejoice:
>and all iniquity shall stop her mouth.

Whoso is wise, and will observe these things,
>even they shall understand the lovingkindness of the Lord.

DELIVERED FROM DEATH
Psalm 116

I love the Lord, because he hath heard my voice
>and my supplications.
Because he hath inclined his ear unto me,
>therefore will I call upon him as long as I live.

The sorrows of death compassed me,
>and the pains of hell gat hold upon me:
>I found trouble and sorrow.
Then called I upon the name of the Lord;
>O Lord, I beseech thee, deliver my soul.

Gracious is the Lord, and righteous;
  yea, our God is merciful.
The Lord preserveth the simple:
  I was brought low, and he helped me.

Return unto thy rest, O my soul;
  for the Lord hath dealt bountifully with thee.

For thou hast delivered my soul from death,
  mine eyes from tears,
  and my feet from falling.
I will walk before the Lord
  in the land of the living.
I believed, therefore have I spoken:
  I was greatly afflicted:
I said in my haste,
  'All men are liars.'

What shall I render unto the Lord
  for all his benefits toward me?
I will take the cup of salvation,
  and call upon the name of the Lord.
I will pay my vows unto the Lord now
  in the presence of all his people.

Precious in the sight of the Lord
  is the death of his saints.
O Lord, truly I am thy servant;
  I am thy servant, and the son of thine handmaid:
  thou hast loosed my bonds.

I will offer to thee the sacrifice of thanksgiving,
  and will call upon the name of the Lord.
I will pay my vows unto the Lord now
  in the presence of all his people,
in the courts of the Lord's house,
  in the midst of thee, O Jerusalem.

Praise ye the Lord.

GOD'S ENDURING MERCY
Psalm 118

O give thanks unto the Lord; for he is good:
   because his mercy endureth for ever.

Let Israel now say,
   that his mercy endureth for ever.
Let the house of Aaron now say,
   that his mercy endureth for ever.
Let them now that fear the Lord say,
   that his mercy endureth for ever.

I called upon the Lord in distress:
   the Lord answered me, and set me in a large place.
The Lord is on my side; I will not fear:
   what can man do unto me?
The Lord taketh my part with them that help me:
   therefore shall I see my desire upon them that hate me.

It is better to trust in the Lord
   than to put confidence in man.
It is better to trust in the Lord
   than to put confidence in princes.

All nations compassed me about:
   but in the name of the Lord will I destroy them.
They compassed me about; yea, they compassed me about:
   but in the name of the Lord I will destroy them.
They compassed me about like bees;
   they are quenched as the fire of thorns:
   for in the name of the Lord I will destroy them.

Thou hast thrust sore at me that I might fall:
   but the Lord helped me.
The Lord is my strength and song,
   and is become my salvation.

The voice of rejoicing and salvation
   is in the tabernacles of the righteous:
   the right hand of the Lord doeth valiantly.

The right hand of the Lord is exalted:
    the right hand of the Lord doeth valiantly.
I shall not die, but live,
    and declare the works of the Lord.
The Lord hath chastened me sore:
    but he hath not given me over unto death.

Open to me the gates of righteousness:
    I will go into them, and I will praise the Lord:
this gate of the Lord,
    into which the righteous shall enter.
I will praise thee: for thou hast heard me,
    and art become my salvation.

The stone which the builders refused
    is become the head stone of the corner.
This is the Lord's doing;
    it is marvellous in our eyes.
This is the day which the Lord hath made;
    we will rejoice and be glad in it.

Save now, I beseech thee, O Lord:
    O Lord, I beseech thee, send now prosperity.
Blessed be he that cometh in the name of the Lord:
    we have blessed you out of the house of the Lord.
God is the Lord,
    which hath shewed us light:
bind the sacrifice with cords,
    even unto the horns of the altar.

Thou art my God, and I will praise thee:
    thou art my God, I will exalt thee.

O give thanks unto the Lord; for he is good:
    for his mercy endureth for ever.

STRENGTHENED BY GOD
Psalm 138

I will praise thee with my whole heart:
    before the gods will I sing praise unto thee.
I will worship toward thy holy temple,
    and praise thy name for thy lovingkindness and for
        thy truth:
    for thou hast magnified thy word above all thy name.
In the day when I cried thou answeredst me,
    and strengthenedst me with strength in my soul.

All the kings of the earth shall praise thee, O Lord,
    when they hear the words of thy mouth.
Yea, they shall sing in the ways of the Lord:
    for great is the glory of the Lord.

Though the Lord be high, yet hath he respect unto the lowly:
    but the proud he knoweth afar off.
Though I walk in the midst of trouble, thou wilt revive me:
    thou shalt stretch forth thine hand against the wrath
        of mine enemies,
    and thy right hand shall save me.
The Lord will perfect that which concerneth me:
    thy mercy, O Lord, endureth for ever:
    forsake not the works of thine own hands.

Part Four

Zion Hymns

GOD IS WITH US
Psalm 46

God is our refuge and strength,
    a very present help in trouble.
Therefore will not we fear, though the earth be removed,
    and though the mountains be carried into the midst of
        the sea;
though the waters thereof roar and be troubled,
    though the mountains shake with the swelling thereof.

There is a river, the streams whereof shall make glad the city
      of God,
    the holy place of the tabernacles of the most High.
God is in the midst of her; she shall not be moved:
    God shall help her, and that right early.
The heathen raged, the kingdoms were moved:
    he uttered his voice, the earth melted.

The Lord of hosts is with us;
    the God of Jacob is our refuge.

Come, behold the works of the Lord,
    what desolations he hath made in the earth.
He maketh wars to cease unto the end of the earth;
    he breaketh the bow, and cutteth the spear in sunder;
    he burneth the chariot in the fire.
Be still, and know that I am God:
    I will be exalted among the heathen,
    I will be exalted in the earth.

The Lord of hosts is with us;
    the God of Jacob is our refuge.

THE CITY OF GOD
Psalm 48

Great is the Lord, and greatly to be praised
   in the city of our God, in the mountain of his holiness.
Beautiful for situation, the joy of the whole earth,
   is mount Zion, on the sides of the north, the city of
      the great King.
God is known in her palaces for a refuge.

For, lo, the kings were assembled,
   they passed by together.
They saw it, and so they marvelled;
   they were troubled, and hasted away.
Fear took hold upon them there,
   and pain, as of a woman in travail.
Thou breakest the ships of Tarshish
   with an east wind.

As we have heard,
   so have we seen
in the city of the Lord of hosts,
   in the city of our God:
      God will establish it for ever.

We have thought of thy lovingkindness, O God,
   in the midst of thy temple.
According to thy name, O God,
   so is thy praise unto the ends of the earth:
      thy right hand is full of righteousness.
Let mount Zion rejoice,
   let the daughters of Judah be glad,
   because of thy judgments.

Walk about Zion, and go round about her:
   tell the towers thereof.
Mark ye well her bulwarks,
   consider her palaces;
      that ye may tell it to the generation following.
For this God is our God for ever and ever:
   he will be our guide even unto death.

GOD'S FEARFUL JUDGMENT
Psalm 76

In Judah is God known:
  his name is great in Israel.
In Salem also is his tabernacle,
  and his dwelling place in Zion.
There brake he the arrows of the bow,
  the shield, and the sword, and the battle.

Thou art more glorious and excellent
  than the mountains of prey.
The stouthearted are spoiled,
  they have slept their sleep:
and none of the men of might
  have found their hands.
At thy rebuke, O God of Jacob,
  both the chariot and horse are cast into a dead sleep.
Thou, even thou, art to be feared:
  and who may stand in thy sight when once thou art angry?
Thou didst cause judgment to be heard from heaven;
  the earth feared, and was still,
when God arose to judgment,
  to save all the meek of the earth.

Surely the wrath of man shall praise thee:
  the remainder of wrath shalt thou restrain.

Vow, and pay unto the Lord your God:
  let all that be round about him
  bring presents unto him that ought to be feared.
He shall cut off the spirit of princes:
  he is terrible to the kings of the earth.

THE BLESSING OF GOD'S HOUSE
Psalm 84

How amiable are thy tabernacles,
    O Lord of hosts!
My soul longeth, yea, even fainteth
    for the courts of the Lord:
my heart and my flesh crieth out
    for the living God.

Yea, the sparrow hath found an house,
    and the swallow a nest for herself,
    where she may lay her young,
even thine altars,
    O Lord of hosts, my King, and my God.
Blessed are they that dwell in thy house:
    they will be still praising thee.

Blessed is the man whose strength is in thee;
    in whose heart are the ways of them.
Who passing through the valley of Baca make it a well;
    the rain also filleth the pools.
They go from strength to strength,
    every one of them in Zion appeareth before God.
O Lord God of hosts, hear my prayer: give ear,
    O God of Jacob.

Behold, O God our shield,
    and look upon the face of thine anointed.

For a day in thy courts
    is better than a thousand.
I had rather be a doorkeeper in the house of my God,
    than to dwell in the tents of wickedness.
For the Lord God is a sun and shield:
    the Lord will give grace and glory:
no good thing will he withhold
    from them that walk uprightly.
O Lord of hosts,
    blessed is the man that trusteth in thee.

THE CITY OF PEACE
Psalm 122

I was glad when they said unto me,
    Let us go into the house of the Lord.
Our feet shall stand
    within thy gates, O Jerusalem.

Jerusalem is builded as a city
    that is compact together:
whither the tribes go up,
    the tribes of the Lord,
unto the testimony of Israel,
    to give thanks unto the name of the Lord.
For there are set thrones of judgment,
    the thrones of the house of David.
Pray for the peace of Jerusalem:
    they shall prosper that love thee.
Peace be within thy walls,
    and prosperity within thy palaces.
For my brethren and companions' sakes,
    I will now say, Peace be within thee.
Because of the house of the Lord our God
    I will seek thy good.

Part Five
Liturgical Psalms

THE GUEST OF GOD
Psalm 15

O Lord, who shall sojourn in thy tent?
   Who shall dwell on thy holy hill?

He who walks blamelessly,
   and does what is right,
and speaks truth from his heart;
   who does not slander with his tongue,
and does no evil to his friend,
   nor takes up a reproach against his neighbour;
in whose eyes a reprobate is despised,
   but who honours those who fear the Lord;
who swears to his own hurt
   and does not change;
who does not put out his money at interest,
   and does not take a bribe against the innocent.

He who does these things
   shall never be moved.

THE KING OF GLORY
Psalm 24

The earth is the Lord's and the fulness thereof,
   the world and those who dwell therein;
for he has founded it upon the seas,
   and established it upon the rivers.

Who shall ascend the hill of the Lord?
    And who shall stand in his holy place?
He who has clean hands and a pure heart,
    who does not lift up his soul to what is false,
    and does not swear deceitfully.
He will receive blessing from the Lord,
    and vindication from the God of his salvation.
Such is the generation of those who seek him,
    who seek the face of the God of Jacob.

Lift up your heads, O gates!
    and be lifted up, O ancient doors!
    that the King of glory may come in.
Who is the King of glory?
    The Lord, strong and mighty,
    the Lord, mighty in battle!
Lift up your heads, O gates!
    and be lifted up, O ancient doors!
    that the King of glory may come in.
Who is this King of glory?
    The Lord of hosts,
    he is the King of glory!

A SACRIFICE OF THANKSGIVING
Psalm 50

The Mighty One, God the Lord,
    speaks and summons the earth
    from the rising of the sun to its setting.
Out of Zion, the perfection of beauty,
    God shines forth.
Our God comes, he does not keep silence,
    before him is a devouring fire,
    round about him a mighty tempest.
He calls to the heavens above
    and to the earth, that he may judge his people:

'Gather to me my faithful ones,
    who made a covenant with me by sacrifice!'
The heavens declare his righteousness,
    for God himself is judge!

'Hear, O my people, and I will speak,
    O Israel, I will testify against you.
    I am God, your God.
I do not reprove you for your sacrifices;
    your burnt offerings are continually before me.
I will accept no bull from your house,
    nor he-goat from your folds.
For every beast of the forest is mine,
    the cattle on a thousand hills.
I know all the birds of the air,
    and all that moves in the field is mine.
If I were hungry, I would not tell you;
    for the world and all that is in it is mine.
Do I eat the flesh of bulls,
    or drink the blood of goats?
Offer to God a sacrifice of thanksgiving,
    and pay your vows to the Most High;
and call upon me in the day of trouble;
    I will deliver you, and you shall glorify me.'

But to the wicked God says:
    'What right have you to recite my statutes,
    or take my covenant on your lips?
For you hate discipline,
    and you cast my words behind you.
If you see a thief, you are a friend of his;
    and you keep company with adulterers.
You give your mouth free rein for evil,
    and your tongue frames deceit.
You sit and speak against your brother;
    you slander your own mother's son.
These things you have done and I have been silent;
    you thought that I was one like yourself.

But now I rebuke you,
    and lay the charge before you.

'Mark this, then, you who forget God,
    lest I rend, and there be none to deliver!
He who brings thanksgiving as his sacrifice honours me;
    to him who orders his way aright
    I will show the salvation of God!'

A NATIONAL SONG OF TRIUMPH
Psalm 68

Let God arise, let his enemies be scattered;
    let those who hate him flee before him!
As smoke is driven away,
    so drive them away;
as wax melts before fire,
    let the wicked perish before God!
But let the righteous be joyful;
    let them exult before God;
    let them be jubilant with joy!

Sing to God, sing praises to his name;
    lift up a song to him who rides upon the clouds;
his name is the Lord,
    exult before him!
Father of the fatherless and protector of widows
    is God in his holy habitation.
God gives the desolate a home to dwell in;
    he leads out the prisoners to prosperity;
    but the rebellious dwell in a parched land.

O God, when thou didst go forth before thy people,
    when thou didst march through the wilderness,
the earth quaked, the heavens poured down rain,
    at the presence of God;
yon Sinai quaked at the presence of God,
    the God of Israel.

Rain in abundance, O God, thou didst shed abroad;
    thou didst restore thy heritage as it languished;
thy flock found a dwelling in it; in thy goodness, O God,
    thou didst provide for the needy.

The Lord gives the command;
    great is the host of those who bore the tidings:
    'The kings of the armies, they flee, they flee!'
The women at home divide the spoil,
    though they stay among the sheepfolds –
the wings of a dove covered with silver,
    its pinions with green gold.
When the Almighty scattered kings there,
    snow fell on Zalmon.

O mighty mountain, mountain of Bashan;
    O many-peaked mountain, mountain of Bashan!
Why look you with envy, O many-peaked mountain,
    at the mount which God desired for his abode,
    yea, where the Lord will dwell for ever?
With mighty chariotry, twice ten thousand,
    thousands upon thousands,
    the Lord came from Sinai into the holy place.
Thou didst ascend the high mount,
    leading captives in thy train,
    and receiving gifts among men,
even among the rebellious,
    that the Lord God may dwell there.

Blessed be the Lord, who daily bears us up;
    God is our salvation.
Our God is a God of salvation;
    and to God, the Lord, belongs escape from death.

But God will shatter the heads of his enemies,
    the hairy crown of him who walks in his guilty ways.
The Lord said, 'I will bring them back from Bashan,
    I will bring them back from the depths of the sea,

that you may bathe your feet in blood,
    that the tongues of your dogs may have their portion
        from the foe.'

Thy solemn processions are seen, O God,
    the processions of my God, my King, into the sanctuary –
the singers in front, the minstrels last,
    between them maidens playing timbrels:
'Bless God in the great congregation,
    the Lord, O you who are of Israel's fountain!'
There is Benjamin, the least of them, in the lead,
    the princes of Judah in their throng,
    the princes of Zebulun, the princes of Naphtali.

Summon thy might, O God;
    show thy strength, O God, thou who hast wrought for us.
Because of thy temple at Jerusalem
    kings bear gifts to thee.
Rebuke the beasts that dwell among the reeds,
    the herd of bulls with the calves of the peoples.
Trample under foot those who lust after tribute;
    scatter the peoples who delight in war.
Let bronze be brought from Egypt;
    let Ethiopia hasten to stretch out her hands to God.

Sing to God, O kingdoms of the earth;
    sing praises to the Lord,
to him who rides in the heavens, the ancient heavens;
    lo, he sends forth his voice, his mighty voice.
Ascribe power to God,
    whose majesty is over Israel,
    and his power is in the skies.
Terrible is God in his sanctuary,
    the God of Israel, he gives power and strength to his
        people.

Blessed be God!

THE GOD OF JUSTICE
Psalm 82

God has taken his place in the divine council;
  in the midst of the gods he holds judgment:

'How long will you judge unjustly
  and show partiality to the wicked?

Give justice to the weak and the fatherless;
  maintain the right of the afflicted and the destitute.
Rescue the weak and the needy;
  deliver them from the hand of the wicked.'

They have neither knowledge nor understanding,
  they walk about in darkness;
  all the foundations of the earth are shaken.

I say, 'You are gods,
  sons of the Most High, all of you;
nevertheless, you shall die like men,
  and fall like any prince.'

Arise, O God, judge the earth;
  for to thee belong all the nations!

THE ONE TRUE GOD
Psalm 115

Not to us, O Lord, not to us,
  but to thy name give glory,
  for the sake of thy steadfast love and thy faithfulness!

Why should the nations say,
  'Where is their God?'
Our God is in the heavens;
  he does whatever he pleases.
Their idols are silver and gold,
  the work of men's hands.

They have mouths, but do not speak;
    eyes, but do not see.
They have ears, but do not hear;
    noses, but do not smell.
They have hands, but do not feel;
    feet, but do not walk;
    and they do not make a sound in their throat.
Those who make them are like them;
    so are all who trust in them.

O Israel, trust in the Lord!
    He is their help and their shield.
O house of Aaron, put your trust in the Lord!
    He is their help and their shield.
You who fear the Lord, trust in the Lord!
    He is their help and their shield.

The Lord has been mindful of us;
    he will bless us; he will bless the house of Israel;
    he will bless the house of Aaron;
he will bless those who fear the Lord,
    both small and great.

May the Lord give you increase,
    you and your children!
May you be blessed by the Lord,
    who made heaven and earth!

The heavens are the Lord's heavens,
    but the earth he has given to the sons of men.
The dead do not praise the Lord,
    nor do any that go down into silence.
But we will bless the Lord
    from this time forth and for evermore.

Praise the Lord!

Part Six

Royal Psalms of Yahweh

YAHWEH'S SPLENDOUR
Psalm 29

Give Yahweh his due, sons of God,
  give Yahweh his due of glory and strength,
give Yahweh the glory due to his name,
  adore Yahweh in the splendour of holiness.

Yahweh's voice over the waters,
  the God of glory thunders;
  Yahweh over countless waters,
Yahweh's voice in power,
  Yahweh's voice in splendour;
Yahweh's voice shatters cedars,
  Yahweh shatters cedars of Lebanon,
he makes Lebanon skip like a calf,
  Sirion like a young wild ox.
Yahweh's voice carves out lightning-shafts,
  Yahweh's voice convulses the desert,
  Yahweh convulses the desert of Kadesh,
Yahweh's voice convulses terebinths,
  strips forests bare.

In his palace all cry, 'Glory!'
Yahweh was enthroned for the flood,
  Yahweh is enthroned as king for ever.
Yahweh will give strength to his people,
  Yahweh blesses his people with peace.

YAHWEH'S ANGER
Psalm 95

Come, let us cry out with joy to Yahweh,
    acclaim the rock of our salvation.
Let us come into his presence with thanksgiving,
    acclaim him with music.

For Yahweh is a great God,
    a king greater than all the gods.
In his power are the depths of the earth,
    the peaks of the mountains are his;
the sea belongs to him, for he made it,
    and the dry land, moulded by his hands.

Come, let us bow low and do reverence;
    kneel before Yahweh who made us!
For he is our God,
    and we the people of his sheepfold,
    the flock of his hand.

If only you would listen to him today!
    Do not harden your hearts as at Meribah,
    as at the time of Massah in the desert,
when your ancestors challenged me,
    put me to the test, and saw what I could do!
For forty years that generation sickened me,
    and I said, 'Always fickle hearts;
    they cannot grasp my ways.'
Then in my anger I swore
    they would never enter my place of rest.

YAHWEH'S SAVING JUSTICE
Psalm 96

Sing a new song to Yahweh!
    Sing to Yahweh, all the earth!
Sing to Yahweh, bless his name!
    Proclaim his salvation day after day,
declare his glory among the nations,
    his marvels to every people!

Great is Yahweh, worthy of all praise,
    more awesome than any of the gods.
All the gods of the nations are idols!
    It was Yahweh who made the heavens;
in his presence are splendour and majesty,
    in his sanctuary power and beauty.

Give to Yahweh, families of nations,
    give to Yahweh glory and power,
    give to Yahweh the glory due to his name!
Bring an offering and enter his courts,
    adore Yahweh in the splendour of his holiness.
Tremble before him, all the earth.

Say among the nations, 'Yahweh is king.'
    The world is set firm, it cannot be moved.
    He will judge the nations with justice.
Let the heavens rejoice and earth be glad!
    Let the sea thunder, and all it holds!
Let the countryside exult, and all that is in it,
    and all the trees of the forest cry out for joy,
at Yahweh's approach, for he is coming,
    coming to judge the earth;
he will judge the world with saving justice,
    and the nations with constancy.

YAHWEH'S TRANSCENDENT GLORY
Psalm 97

Yahweh is king! Let earth rejoice,
    the many isles be glad!
Cloud, black cloud enfolds him,
    saving justice and judgment the foundations of his throne.

Fire goes before him,
    sets ablaze his enemies all around;
his lightning-flashes light up the world,
    the earth sees it and quakes.

The mountains melt like wax,
    before the Lord of all the earth.
The heavens proclaim his saving justice,
    all nations see his glory.

Shame on all who serve images,
    who pride themselves on their idols;
    bow down to him, all you gods!

Zion hears and is glad,
    the daughters of Judah exult,
    because of your judgments, Yahweh.

For you are Yahweh,
    Most High over all the earth,
    far transcending all gods.

Yahweh loves those who hate evil,
    he keeps safe his faithful,
    rescues them from the clutches of the wicked.

Light dawns for the upright,
    and joy for honest hearts.
Rejoice in Yahweh, you who are upright,
    praise his unforgettable holiness.

YAHWEH'S SAVING POWER
Psalm 98

Sing a new song to Yahweh,
    for he has performed wonders,
his saving power is in his right hand
    and his holy arm.

Yahweh has made known his saving power,
    revealed his saving justice for the nations to see,
mindful of his faithful love
    and his constancy to the House of Israel.
The whole wide world has seen
    the saving power of our God.

Acclaim Yahweh, all the earth,
    burst into shouts of joy!
Play to Yahweh on the harp,
    to the sound of instruments;
to the sound of trumpet and horn,
    acclaim the presence of the King.

Let the sea thunder, and all that it holds,
    the world and all who live in it.
Let the rivers clap their hands,
    and the mountains shout for joy together,
    at Yahweh's approach,
    for he is coming to judge the earth;
he will judge the world with saving justice
    and the nations with fairness.

Part Seven

Royal Psalms of the King

YAHWEH'S ANOINTED SON
Psalm 2

Why this uproar among the nations,
    this impotent muttering of the peoples?
Kings of the earth take up position,
    princes plot together
    against Yahweh and his anointed,
'Now let us break their fetters!
    Now let us throw off their bonds!'

He who is enthroned in the heavens laughs,
    Yahweh makes a mockery of them,
then in his anger rebukes them,
    in his rage he strikes them with terror.
'I myself have anointed my king
    on Zion my holy mountain.'

I will proclaim the decree of Yahweh:

He said to me, 'You are my son,
    today have I fathered you.
Ask of me,
    and I shall give you the nations as your birthright,
    the whole wide world as your possession.
With an iron sceptre you will break them,
    shatter them like so many pots.'

So now, you kings, come to your senses,
    you earthly rulers, learn your lesson!
In fear be submissive to Yahweh;
    with trembling kiss his feet,

lest he be angry and your way come to nothing,
    for his fury flares up in a moment.
How blessed are all those who take refuge in him!

YAHWEH, THE KING'S PROTECTOR
Psalm 18

I love you, Yahweh, my strength
    (my Saviour, you have saved me from violence).

Yahweh is my rock and my fortress,
    my deliverer is my God.
I take refuge in him, my rock,
    my shield, my saving strength,
    my stronghold, my place of refuge.
I call to Yahweh who is worthy of praise,
    and I am saved from my foes.

With Death's breakers closing in on me,
    Belial's torrents ready to swallow me,
Sheol's snares every side of me,
    Death's traps lying ahead of me,
I called to Yahweh in my anguish,
    I cried for help to my God;
from his Temple he heard my voice,
    my cry came to his ears.

Then the earth quaked and rocked,
    the mountains' foundations shuddered,
    they quaked at his blazing anger.
Smoke rose from his nostrils,
    from his mouth devouring fire
    (coals were kindled at it).
He parted the heavens and came down,
    a storm-cloud underneath his feet;
riding one of the winged creatures, he flew,
    soaring on the wings of the wind.

His covering he made the darkness,
    his pavilion dark waters and dense cloud.
A brightness lit up before him,
    hail and blazing fire.
Yahweh thundered from the heavens,
    the Most High made his voice heard.
He shot his arrows and scattered them,
    he hurled his lightning and routed them.
The very springs of ocean were exposed,
    the world's foundations were laid bare,
at your roaring, Yahweh,
    at the blast of breath from your nostrils!

He reached down from on high, snatched me up,
    pulled me from the watery depths,
rescued me from my mighty foe,
    from my enemies who were stronger than I.
They assailed me on my day of disaster
    but Yahweh was there to support me;
he freed me, set me at large,
    he rescued me because he loves me.

Yahweh rewards me for my uprightness,
    as my hands are pure, so he repays me,
since I have kept the ways of Yahweh,
    and not fallen away from my God.
His judgments are all before me,
    his statutes I have not put away from me.
I am blameless before him,
    I keep myself clear of evil.
So Yahweh repaid me for acting uprightly
    because he could see I was pure.

You are faithful to the faithful,
    blameless with the blameless,
sincere to the sincere,
    but cunning to the crafty,
you save a people that is humble
    and humiliate those with haughty looks.

Yahweh, you yourself are my lamp,
    my God lights up my darkness;
with you I storm the rampart,
    with my God I can scale any wall.

This God, his way is blameless;
    the word of Yahweh is refined in the furnace,
    for he alone is the shield of all who take refuge in him.
For who is God but Yahweh,
    who is a rock but our God?
This God who girds me with strength,
    who makes my way free from blame,
who makes me as swift as a deer
    and sets me firmly on the heights,
who trains my hands for battle,
    my arms to bend a bow of bronze.
You give me your invincible shield
    (your right hand upholds me)
    you never cease to listen to me,
you give me the strides of a giant,
    give me ankles that never weaken.

I pursue my enemies and overtake them,
    not turning back till they are annihilated;
I strike them down and they cannot rise,
    they fall, they are under my feet.
You have girded me with strength for the fight,
    bent down my assailants beneath me,
made my enemies retreat before me;
    and those who hate me I destroy.
They cry out, there is no one to save;
    to Yahweh, but no answer comes.
I crumble them like dust before the wind,
    trample them like the mud of the streets.

You free me from the quarrels of my people,
    you place me at the head of the nations,
    a people I did not know are now my servants;

foreigners come wooing my favour,
    no sooner do they hear than they obey me;
foreigners grow faint of heart,
    they come trembling out of their fastnesses.

Life to Yahweh! Blessed be my rock!
    Exalted be the God of my salvation,
the God who gives me vengeance,
    and subjects whole peoples to me,
    who rescues me from my raging enemies.
You lift me high above those who attack me,
    you deliver me from the man of violence.
For this I will praise you, Yahweh, among the nations,
    and sing praise to your name.
He saves his king time after time,
    displays his faithful love for his anointed,
    for David and his heirs for ever.

BLESSINGS ON YAHWEH'S KING
Psalm 20

May Yahweh answer you in time of trouble,
    may the name of the God of Jacob protect you!
May he send you help from the sanctuary,
    give you support from Zion!
May he remember all your sacrifices
    and delight in your burnt offerings!

May he grant you your heart's desire
    and crown all your plans with success!
So that with joy we can hail your victory
    and draw up our ranks in the name of our God.
May Yahweh grant all your petitions.

Now I know that Yahweh gives victory to his anointed.
    He will respond from his holy heavens
    with great deeds of victory from his right hand.

Some call on chariots, some on horses,
    but we on the name of Yahweh our God.
They will crumple and fall,
    while we stand upright and firm.

Yahweh, save the king,
    answer us when we call.

A WEDDING SONG
Psalm 45

My heart is stirred by a noble theme,
    I address my poem to the king,
    my tongue the pen of an expert scribe.

Of all men you are the most handsome,
    gracefulness is a dew upon your lips,
    for God has blessed you for ever.
Warrior, strap your sword at your side,
    in your majesty and splendour advance, ride on
    in the cause of truth, gentleness and uprightness.
Stretch the bowstring tight,
    lending terror to your right hand.
Your arrows are sharp, nations lie at your mercy,
    the king's enemies lose heart.
Your throne is from God, for ever and ever,
    the sceptre of your kingship a sceptre of justice,
    you love uprightness and detest evil.
This is why God, your God, has anointed you with oil
        of gladness,
    as none of your rivals,
    your robes all myrrh and aloes.
From palaces of ivory, harps bring you joy,
    in your retinue are daughters of kings,
    the consort at your right hand in gold of Ophir.

Listen, my daughter, attend to my words and hear;
    forget your own nation and your ancestral home,

then the king will fall in love with your beauty;
    he is your lord, bow down before him.
The daughter of Tyre will court your favour with gifts,
    and the richest of peoples with jewels set in gold.

Clothed in brocade, the king's daughter is led within
    to the king with the maidens of her retinue;
her companions are brought to her,
    they enter the king's palace with joy and rejoicing.
Instead of your ancestors you will have sons;
    you will make them rulers over the whole world.
I will make your name endure from generation to generation,
    so nations will sing your praise for ever and ever.

A VISION OF JUSTICE AND PEACE
Psalm 72

God, endow the king with your own fair judgment,
    the son of the king with your own saving justice,
that he may rule your people with justice,
    and your poor with fair judgment.

Mountains and hills, bring peace to the people!
With justice he will judge the poor of the people,
    he will save the children of the needy
    and crush their oppressors.

In the sight of the sun and the moon
    he will endure, age after age.
He will come down like rain on mown grass,
    like showers moistening the land.
In his days uprightness shall flourish,
    and peace in plenty till the moon is no more.

His empire shall stretch from sea to sea,
    from the river to the limits of the earth.
The Beast will cower before him,
    his enemies lick the dust;

the kings of Tarshish and the islands will pay him tribute.
    The kings of Sheba and Saba will offer gifts;
all kings will do him homage,
    all nations become his servants.

For he rescues anyone needy who calls to him,
    and the poor who has no one to help.
He has pity on the weak and the needy,
    and saves the needy from death.
From oppression and violence he redeems their lives,
    their blood is precious in his sight.

(Long may he live;
    may the gold of Sheba be given him!)
Prayer will be offered for him constantly,
    and blessings invoked on him all day.
May wheat abound in the land,
    waving on the heights of the hills,
like Lebanon with its fruits and flowers at their best,
    like the grasses of the earth.
May his name be blessed for ever,
    and endure in the sight of the sun.

In him shall be blessed every race in the world,
    and all nations call him blessed.

WHERE IS YAHWEH'S LOVE?
Psalm 89

I shall sing the faithful love of Yahweh for ever,
    from age to age my lips shall declare your constancy,
for you have said: love is built to last for ever,
    you have fixed your constancy firm in the heavens.

'I have made a covenant with my Chosen One,
    sworn an oath to my servant David:
I have made your dynasty firm for ever,
    built your throne stable age after age.'

The heavens praise your wonders, Yahweh,
    your constancy in the gathering of your faithful.
Who in the skies can compare with Yahweh?
    Who among the sons of god can rival him?
God, awesome in the assembly of holy ones,
    great and dreaded among all who surround him,
Yahweh, God Sabaoth, who is like you?
    Mighty Yahweh, your constancy is all round you!

You control the pride of the ocean,
    when its waves ride high you calm them.
You split Rahab in two like a corpse,
    scattered your enemies with your mighty arm.
Yours are the heavens and yours the earth,
    the world and all it holds, you founded them;
you created the north and the south,
    Tabor and Hermon hail your name with joy.
Yours is a strong arm, mighty your hand,
    your right hand raised high;

Saving Justice and Fair Judgment the foundations of your
      throne,
    Faithful Love and Constancy march before you.
How blessed the nation that learns to acclaim you!
    They will live, Yahweh, in the light of your presence.
In your name they rejoice all day long,
    by your saving justice they are raised up.
You are the flower of their strength,
    by your favour our strength is triumphant;
for to Yahweh belongs our shield,
    to the Holy One of Israel our king.

Once you spoke in a vision,
    to your faithful you said:
'I have given strength to a warrior,
    I have raised up a man chosen from my people.
I have found David my servant,
    and anointed him with my holy oil.

My hand will always be with him,
    my arm will make him strong.
No enemy will be able to outwit him,
    no wicked man overcome him;
I shall crush his enemies before him,
    strike his opponents dead.
My constancy and faithful love will be with him,
    in my name his strength will be triumphant.
I shall establish his power over the sea,
    his dominion over the rivers.
He will cry to me, "You are my father,
    my God, the rock of my salvation!"
So I shall make him my first-born,
    the highest of earthly kings.
I shall maintain my faithful love for him always,
    my covenant with him will stay firm.
I have established his dynasty for ever,
    his throne to be as lasting as the heavens.

'Should his descendants desert my law,
    and not keep to my rulings,
should they violate my statutes,
    and not observe my commandments,
then I shall punish their offences with the rod,
    their guilt with the whip,
but I shall never withdraw from him my faithful love,
    I shall not belie my constancy.
I shall not violate my covenant,
    I shall not withdraw the word once spoken.
I have sworn by my holiness, once and for all,
    never will I break faith with David.
His dynasty shall endure for ever,
    his throne like the sun before me,
as the moon is established for ever,
    a faithful witness in the skies.'

Yet you yourself – you have spurned and rejected,
    and have vented your wrath on your anointed,

you have repudiated the covenant with your servant,
    dishonoured his crown in the dust.
You have pierced all his defences,
    and laid his strongholds in ruins,
everyone passing by plunders him,
    he has become the butt of his neighbours.
You have raised high the right hand of his opponents,
    have made all his enemies happy;
you have snapped off his sword on a rock,
    and failed to support him in battle.
You have stripped him of his splendid sceptre,
    and toppled his throne to the ground.
You have aged him before his time,
    enveloped him in shame.

How long, Yahweh, will you remain hidden? For ever?
    Is your anger to go on smouldering like a fire?
Remember me; how long have I left?
    For what pointless end did you create all the children
        of Adam?
Who can live and never see death?
    Who can save himself from the clutches of Sheol?
Lord, what of those pledges of your faithful love?
    You made an oath to David by your constancy.
Do not forget the insults to your servant;
    I take to heart the taunts of the nations,
which your enemies have levelled, Yahweh,
    have levelled at the footsteps of your anointed!

YAHWEH'S PRIEST AND KING
Psalm 110

Yahweh declared to my Lord,
    'Take your seat at my right hand,
    till I have made your enemies your footstool.'

Yahweh will stretch out the sceptre of your power;
    from Zion you will rule your foes all around you.

Royal dignity has been yours from the day of your birth,
    sacred honour from the womb, from the dawn of your
        youth.

Yahweh has sworn an oath he will never retract,
    you are a priest for ever of the order of Melchizedek.

At your right hand, Lord,
    he shatters kings when his anger breaks out.
He judges nations, heaping up corpses,
    he breaks heads over the whole wide world.
He drinks from a stream as he goes,
    and therefore he holds his head high.

BLESSINGS ON YAHWEH'S PEOPLE
Psalm 144

Blessed be Yahweh, my rock,
    who trains my hands for war
    and my fingers for battle,
my faithful love, my bastion,
    my citadel, my Saviour;
I shelter behind him, my shield,
    he makes the peoples submit to me.

Yahweh, what is a human being for you to notice,
    a child of Adam for you to think about?
Human life, a mere puff of wind,
    days as fleeting as a shadow.

Yahweh, part the heavens and come down,
    touch the mountains, make them smoke.
Scatter them with continuous lightning-flashes,
    rout them with a volley of your arrows.
Stretch down your hand from above,
    save me, rescue me from deep waters,
    from the clutches of foreigners,
whose every word is worthless,
    whose right hand is raised in perjury.

God, I sing to you a new song,
    I play to you on the ten-stringed lyre,
for you give kings their victories,
    you rescue your servant David.
From the sword of evil save me,
    rescue me from the clutches of foreigners
whose every word is worthless,
    whose right hand testifies to falsehood.

May our sons be like plants
    growing tall from their earliest days,
our daughters like pillars
    carved fit for a palace,
our barns filled to overflowing
    with every kind of crop,
the sheep in our pastures be numbered
    in thousands and tens of thousands,
our cattle well fed, free of raids and pillage,
    free of outcry in our streets.

How blessed the nation of whom this is true,
    blessed the nation whose God is Yahweh!

Part Eight

Individual Laments

AT PEACE WITH GOD
Psalm 4

Answer me when I call,
  O God of my right!
Thou hast given me room when I was in distress.
  Be gracious to me, and hear my prayer.

O men, how long shall my honour suffer shame?
  How long will you love vain words, and seek after lies?
But know that the Lord has set apart the godly for himself;
  the Lord hears when I call to him.

Be angry, but sin not;
  commune with your own hearts on your beds, and be
    silent.

Offer right sacrifices,
  and put your trust in the Lord.

There are many who say, 'O that we might see some good!
  Lift up the light of thy countenance upon us, O Lord!'
Thou hast put more joy in my heart
  than they have when their grain and wine abound.
In peace I will both lie down and sleep;
  for thou alone, O Lord,
    makest me dwell in safety.

LEAD ME IN THY RIGHTEOUSNESS
Psalm 5

Give ear to my words, O Lord;
   give heed to my groaning.
Hearken to the sound of my cry,
   my King and my God,
   for to thee do I pray.
O Lord, in the morning thou dost hear my voice;
   in the morning I prepare a sacrifice for thee, and watch.

For thou art not a God who delights in wickedness;
   evil may not sojourn with thee.
The boastful may not stand before thy eyes;
   thou hatest all evildoers.
Thou destroyest those who speak lies;
   the Lord abhors bloodthirsty and deceitful men.

But I through the abundance of thy steadfast love
   will enter thy house,
I will worship toward thy holy temple
   in the fear of thee.
Lead me, O Lord, in thy righteousness
   because of my enemies;
   make thy way straight before me.

For there is no truth in their mouth;
   their heart is destruction,
their throat is an open sepulchre,
   they flatter with their tongue.
Make them bear their guilt, O God;
   let them fall by their own counsels;
because of their many transgressions cast them out,
   for they have rebelled against thee.

But let all who take refuge in thee rejoice,
   let them ever sing for joy;
and do thou defend them,
   that those who love thy name may exult in thee.

For thou dost bless the righteous, O Lord;
  thou dost cover him with favour as with a shield.

PRAYER FROM A TROUBLED SOUL
Psalm 6

O Lord, rebuke me not in thy anger,
  nor chasten me in thy wrath.
Be gracious to me, O Lord, for I am languishing;
  O Lord, heal me, for my bones are troubled.
My soul also is sorely troubled.
  But thou, O Lord – how long?

Turn, O Lord, save my life;
  deliver me for the sake of thy steadfast love.
For in death there is no remembrance of thee;
  in Sheol who can give thee praise?

I am weary with my moaning;
  every night I flood my bed with tears;
  I drench my couch with my weeping.
My eye wastes away because of grief,
  it grows weak because of all my foes.

Depart from me, all you workers of evil;
  for the Lord has heard the sound of my weeping.
The Lord has heard my supplication;
  the Lord accepts my prayer.
All my enemies shall be ashamed and sorely troubled;
  they shall turn back, and be put to shame in a moment.

AN APPEAL TO GOD'S JUSTICE
Psalm 7

O Lord my God, in thee do I take refuge;
  save me from all my pursuers, and deliver me,

lest like a lion they rend me,
    dragging me away, with none to rescue.

O Lord my God, if I have done this,
    if there is wrong in my hands,
if I have requited my friend with evil
    or plundered my enemy without cause,
let the enemy pursue me and overtake me,
    and let him trample my life to the ground,
    and lay my soul in the dust.

Arise, O Lord, in thy anger,
    lift thyself up against the fury of my enemies;
    awake, O my God; thou hast appointed a judgment.
Let the assembly of the peoples be gathered about thee;
    and over it take thy seat on high.
The Lord judges the peoples;
    judge me, O Lord, according to my righteousness
    and according to the integrity that is in me.

O let the evil of the wicked come to an end,
    but establish thou the righteous,
thou who triest the minds and hearts,
    thou righteous God.
My shield is with God,
    who saves the upright in heart.
God is a righteous judge,
    and a God who has indignation every day.

If a man does not repent,
    God will whet his sword;
    he has bent and strung his bow;
he has prepared his deadly weapons,
    making his arrows fiery shafts.
Behold, the wicked man conceives evil,
    and is pregnant with mischief,
    and brings forth lies.
He makes a pit, digging it out,
    and falls into the hole which he has made.

His mischief returns upon his own head,
    and on his own pate his violence descends.

I will give to the Lord the thanks due to his righteousness,
    and I will sing praise to the name of the Lord,
        the Most High.

HOPE OF THE POOR
Psalm 9

I will give thanks to the Lord with my whole heart;
    I will tell of all thy wonderful deeds.
I will be glad and exult in thee,
    I will sing praise to thy name, O Most High.

When my enemies turned back,
    they stumbled and perished before thee.
For thou hast maintained my just cause;
    thou hast sat on the throne giving righteous judgment.
Thou hast rebuked the nations, thou hast destroyed the wicked;
    thou hast blotted out their name for ever and ever.
The enemy have vanished in everlasting ruins;
    their cities thou hast rooted out;
    the very memory of them has perished.
But the Lord sits enthroned for ever,
    he has established his throne for judgment;
and he judges the world with righteousness,
    he judges the peoples with equity.
The Lord is a stronghold for the oppressed,
    a stronghold in times of trouble.
And those who know thy name put their trust in thee,
    for thou, O Lord, hast not forsaken those who seek thee.

Sing praises to the Lord, who dwells in Zion!
    Tell among the peoples his deeds!
For he who avenges blood is mindful of them;
    he does not forget the cry of the afflicted.

Be gracious to me, O Lord!
  Behold what I suffer from those who hate me,
  O thou who liftest me up from the gates of death,
that I may recount all thy praises,
  that in the gates of the daughter of Zion
  I may rejoice in thy deliverance.
The nations have sunk in the pit which they made;
  in the net which they hid has their own foot been caught.
The Lord has made himself known, he has executed
    judgment;
  the wicked are snared in the work of their own hands.

The wicked shall depart to Sheol,
  all the nations that forget God.
For the needy shall not always be forgotten,
  and the hope of the poor shall not perish for ever.

Arise, O Lord! Let not man prevail;
  let the nations be judged before thee!
Put them in fear, O Lord!
  Let the nations know that they are but men!

DESIRE OF THE MEEK
Psalm 10

Why dost thou stand afar off, O Lord?
  Why dost thou hide thyself in times of trouble?

In arrogance the wicked hotly pursue the poor;
  let them be caught in the schemes which they have devised.
For the wicked boasts of the desires of his heart,
  and the man greedy for gain curses and renounces the Lord.
In the pride of his countenance the wicked does not seek him;
  all his thoughts are, 'There is no God.'
His ways prosper at all times;
  thy judgments are on high, out of his sight;
  as for all his foes, he puffs at them.

He thinks in his heart, 'I shall not be moved;
  throughout all generations I shall not meet adversity.'
His mouth is filled with cursing and deceit and oppression;
  under his tongue are mischief and iniquity.
He sits in ambush in the villages;
  in hiding places he murders the innocent.
His eyes stealthily watch for the hapless,
  he lurks in secret like a lion in his covert;
he lurks that he may seize the poor,
  he seizes the poor when he draws him into his net.
The hapless is crushed, sinks down,
  and falls by his might.
He thinks in his heart, 'God has forgotten,
  he has hidden his face, he will never see it.'

Arise, O Lord; O God, lift up thy hand;
  forget not the afflicted.
Why does the wicked renounce God, and say in his heart,
  'Thou wilt not call to account'?
Thou dost see; yea, thou dost note trouble and vexation,
  that thou mayst take it into thy hands;
the hapless commits himself to thee;
  thou hast been the helper of the fatherless.
Break thou the arm of the wicked and evildoer;
  seek out his wickedness till thou find none.

The Lord is king for ever and ever;
  the nations shall perish from his land.
O Lord, thou wilt hear the desire of the meek;
  thou wilt strengthen their heart, thou wilt incline thy ear
to do justice to the fatherless and the oppressed,
  so that man who is of the earth may strike terror no more.

CRY TO A HIDDEN GOD
Psalm 13

How long, O Lord? Wilt thou forget me for ever?
    How long wilt thou hide thy face from me?
How long must I bear pain in my soul,
    and have sorrow in my heart all the day?
    How long shall my enemy be exalted over me?

Consider and answer me, O Lord my God;
    lighten my eyes, lest I sleep the sleep of death;
lest my enemy say, 'I have prevailed over him';
    lest my foes rejoice because I am shaken.

But I have trusted in thy steadfast love;
    my heart shall rejoice in thy salvation.
I will sing to the Lord,
    because he has dealt bountifully with me.

PRAYER FOR VINDICATION
Psalm 17

Hear a just cause, O Lord; attend to my cry!
    Give ear to my prayer from lips free of deceit!
From thee let my vindication come!
    Let thy eyes see the right!

If thou triest my heart, if thou visitest me by night,
    if thou testest me, thou wilt find no wickedness in me;
    my mouth does not transgress.
With regard to the works of men,
    by the word of thy lips
I have avoided the ways of the violent.
My steps have held fast to thy paths,
    my feet have not slipped.

I call upon thee, for thou wilt answer me, O God;
    incline thy ear to me, hear my words.

Wondrously show thy steadfast love,
  O saviour of those who seek refuge
  from their adversaries at thy right hand.
Keep me as the apple of the eye;
  hide me in the shadow of thy wings,
from the wicked who despoil me,
  my deadly enemies who surround me.

They close their hearts to pity;
  with their mouths they speak arrogantly.
They track me down; now they surround me;
  they set their eyes to cast me to the ground.
They are like a lion eager to tear,
  as a young lion lurking in ambush.

Arise, O Lord! confront them, overthrow them!
  Deliver my life from the wicked by thy sword,
from men by thy hand, O Lord,
  from men whose portion in life is of the world.

May their belly be filled with what thou hast stored up for them;
  may their children have more than enough;
  may they leave something over to their babes.
As for me, I shall behold thy face in righteousness;
  when I awake, I shall be satisfied with beholding thy form.

CRY OF THE GOD-FORSAKEN
Psalm 22

My God, my God, why hast thou forsaken me?
  Why art thou so far from helping me,
  from the words of my groaning?
O my God, I cry by day, but thou dost not answer;
  and by night, but find no rest.

Yet thou art holy, enthroned on the praises of Israel.
  In thee our fathers trusted;
  they trusted, and thou didst deliver them.

To thee they cried, and were saved;
    in thee they trusted, and were not disappointed.

But I am a worm, and no man;
    scorned by men, and despised by the people.
All who see me mock at me,
    they make mouths at me, they wag their heads;
'He committed his cause to the Lord;
    let him deliver him, let him rescue him,
    for he delights in him!'

Yet thou art he who took me from the womb;
    thou didst keep me safe upon my mother's breasts.
Upon thee was I cast from my birth,
    and since my mother bore me thou hast been my God.
Be not far from me,
    for trouble is near and there is none to help.

Many bulls encompass me,
    strong bulls of Bashan surround me;
they open wide their mouths at me,
    like a ravening and roaring lion.
I am poured out like water,
    and all my bones are out of joint;
my heart is like wax,
    it is melted within my breast;
my strength is dried up like a potsherd,
    and my tongue cleaves to my jaws;
    thou dost lay me in the dust of death.
Yea, dogs are round about me;
    a company of evildoers encircle me;
    they have pierced my hands and feet –
I can count all my bones – they stare and gloat over me;
    they divide my garments among them,
    and for my raiment they cast lots.

But thou, O Lord, be not far off!
    O thou my help, hasten to my aid!
Deliver my soul from the sword,
    my life from the power of the dog!

Save me from the mouth of the lion,
    my afflicted soul from the horns of the wild oxen!

I will tell of thy name to my brethren;
    in the midst of the congregation I will praise thee:
You who fear the Lord, praise him!
    all you sons of Jacob, glorify him,
    and stand in awe of him, all you sons of Israel!
For he has not despised or abhorred
    the affliction of the afflicted;
and he has not hid his face from him,
    but has heard, when he cried to him.

From thee comes my praise in the great congregation;
    my vows I will pay before those who fear him.
The afflicted shall eat and be satisfied;
    those who seek him shall praise the Lord!
    May your hearts live for ever!
All the ends of the earth shall remember
    and turn to the Lord;
and all the families of the nations
    shall worship before him.
For dominion belongs to the Lord,
    and he rules over the nations.

Yea, to him shall all the proud of the earth bow down;
    before him shall bow all who go down to the dust,
    and he who cannot keep himself alive.
Posterity shall serve him;
    men shall tell of the Lord to the coming generation,
and proclaim his deliverance to a people yet unborn,
    that he has wrought it.

LEAD ME IN THY TRUTH
Psalm 25

To thee, O Lord, I lift up my soul.
  O my God, in thee I trust,
let me not be put to shame;
  let not my enemies exult over me.
Yea, let none that wait for thee be put to shame;
  let them be ashamed who are wantonly treacherous.

Make me to know thy ways, O Lord;
  teach me thy paths.
Lead me in thy truth, and teach me,
  for thou art the God of my salvation;
  for thee I wait all the day long.
Be mindful of thy mercy, O Lord,
  and of thy steadfast love,
  for they have been from of old.
Remember not the sins of my youth, or my transgressions;
  according to thy steadfast love remember me,
  for thy goodness' sake, O Lord!

Good and upright is the Lord;
  therefore he instructs sinners in the way.
He leads the humble in what is right,
  and teaches the humble his way.
All the paths of the Lord are steadfast love and faithfulness,
  for those who keep his covenant and his testimonies.
For thy name's sake, O Lord,
  pardon my guilt, for it is great.
Who is the man that fears the Lord?
  Him will he instruct in the way that he should choose.
He himself shall abide in prosperity,
  and his children shall possess the land.
The friendship of the Lord is for those who fear him,
  and he makes known to them his covenant.
My eyes are ever towards the Lord,
  for he will pluck my feet out of the net.

Turn thou to me, and be gracious to me;
    for I am lonely and afflicted.
Relieve the troubles of my heart,
    and bring me out of my distresses.
Consider my affliction and my trouble,
    and forgive all my sins.
Consider how many are my foes,
    and with what violent hatred they hate me.
Oh guard my life, and deliver me;
    let me not be put to shame,
    for I take refuge in thee.
May integrity and uprightness preserve me,
    for I wait for thee.

Redeem Israel, O God,
    out of all his troubles.

THE LORD IS MY STRENGTH
Psalm 28

To thee, O Lord, I call;
    my rock, be not deaf to me,
lest, if thou be silent to me,
    I become like those who go down to the Pit.
Hear the voice of my supplication,
    as I cry to thee for help,
as I lift up my hands
    towards thy most holy sanctuary.

Take me not off with the wicked,
    with those who are workers of evil,
who speak peace with their neighbours,
    while mischief is in their hearts.
Requite them according to their work,
    and according to the evil of their deeds;
requite them according to the work of their hands;
    render them their due reward.

Because they do not regard the works of the Lord,
    or the work of his hands,
he will break them down
    and build them up no more.

Blessed be the Lord!
    for he has heard the voice of my supplications.
The Lord is my strength and my shield;
    in him my heart trusts;
so I am helped, and my heart exults,
    and with my song I give thanks to him.

The Lord is the strength of his people,
    he is the saving refuge of his anointed.
O save thy people, and bless thy heritage;
    be thou their shepherd, and carry them for ever.

A CONFESSION
Psalm 38

O Lord, rebuke me not in thy anger,
    nor chasten me in thy wrath!
For thy arrows have sunk into me,
    and thy hand has come down on me.
There is no soundness in my flesh because of thy indignation;
    there is no health in my bones because of my sin.
For my iniquities have gone over my head;
    they weigh like a burden too heavy for me.

My wounds grow foul and fester
    because of my foolishness,
I am utterly bowed down and prostrate;
    all the day I go about mourning.
For my loins are filled with burning,
    and there is no soundness in my flesh.
I am utterly spent and crushed;
    I groan because of the tumult of my heart.

Lord, all my longing is known to thee,
   my sighing is not hidden from thee.
My heart throbs, my strength fails me;
   and the light of my eyes – it also has gone from me.
My friends and companions stand aloof from my plague,
   and my kinsmen stand afar off.
Those who seek my life lay their snares,
   those who seek my hurt speak of ruin,
   and meditate treachery all the day long.

But I am like a deaf man, I do not hear,
   like a dumb man who does not open his mouth.
Yea, I am like a man who does not hear,
   and in whose mouth are no rebukes.
But for thee, O Lord, do I wait;
   it is thou, O Lord my God, who wilt answer.
For I pray, 'Only let them not rejoice over me,
   who boast against me when my foot slips!'

For I am ready to fall,
   and my pain is ever with me.
I confess my iniquity,
   I am sorry for my sin.
Those who are my foes without cause are mighty,
   and many are those who hate me wrongfully.
Those who render me evil for good are my adversaries
   because I follow after good.

Do not forsake me, O Lord!
   O my God, be not far from me!
Make haste to help me,
   O Lord, my salvation!

MAN IS A MERE BREATH
Psalm 39

I said, 'I will guard my ways,
  that I may not sin with my tongue;
I will bridle my mouth,
  so long as the wicked are in my presence.'
I was dumb and silent,
  I held my peace to no avail;
my distress grew worse,
  my heart became hot within me.
As I mused, the fire burned;
  then I spoke with my tongue:

'Lord, let me know my end,
  and what is the measure of my days;
  let me know how fleeting my life is!
Behold, thou hast made my days a few handbreadths,
  and my lifetime is as nothing in thy sight.
  Surely every man stands as a mere breath!
Surely man goes about as a shadow!
  Surely for nought are they in turmoil;
  man heaps up, and knows not who will gather!

'And now, Lord, for what do I wait?
  My hope is in thee.
Deliver me from all my transgressions.
  Make me not the scorn of the fool!
I am dumb, I do not open my mouth;
  for it is thou who hast done it.
Remove thy stroke from me;
  I am spent by the blows of thy hand.
When thou dost chasten man with rebukes for sin,
  thou dost consume like a moth what is dear to him;
  surely every man is a mere breath!

'Hear my prayer, O Lord, and give ear to my cry;
  hold not thy peace at my tears!

For I am thy passing guest,
a sojourner, like all my fathers.
Look away from me, that I may know gladness,
before I depart and be no more!'

THIRSTY FOR GOD
Psalm 42

As a hart longs for flowing streams,
so longs my soul for thee, O God.
My soul thirsts for God, for the living God.
When shall I come and behold the face of God?
My tears have been my food
day and night,
while men say to me continually,
'Where is your God?'
These things I remember,
as I pour out my soul:
how I went with the throng,
and led them in procession to the house of God,
with glad shouts and songs of thanksgiving,
a multitude keeping festival.

Why are you cast down, O my soul,
and why are you disquieted within me?
Hope in God;
for I shall again praise him,
my help and my God.
My soul is cast down within me,
therefore I remember thee
from the land of Jordan and of Hermon,
from Mount Mizar.
Deep calls to deep
at the thunder of thy cataracts;
all thy waves and thy billows
have gone over me.

By day the Lord commands his steadfast love;
    and at night his song is with me,
    a prayer to the God of my life.

I say to God, my rock:
    'Why hast thou forgotten me?
Why go I mourning
    because of the oppression of the enemy?'
As with a deadly wound in my body,
    my adversaries taunt me,
while they say to me continually,
    'Where is your God?'

Why are you cast down, O my soul,
    and why are you disquieted within me?
Hope in God;
    for I shall again praise him,
    my help and my God.

JOY IN GOD
Psalm 43

Vindicate me, O God, and defend my cause
    against an ungodly people;
    from deceitful and unjust men deliver me!
For thou art the God in whom I take refuge;
    why hast thou cast me off?
Why go I mourning
    because of the oppression of the enemy?
Oh send out thy light and thy truth;
    let them lead me,
let them bring me to thy holy hill
    and to thy dwelling!
Then I will go to the altar of God,
    to God my exceeding joy;
and I will praise thee with the lyre,
    O God, my God.

Why are you cast down, O my soul,
    and why are you disquieted within me?
Hope in God;
    for I shall again praise him,
    my help and my God.

SONG OF A CONTRITE HEART
Psalm 51

Have mercy on me, O God,
    according to thy steadfast love;
according to thy abundant mercy
    blot out my transgressions.
Wash me thoroughly from my iniquity,
    and cleanse me from my sin!

For I know my transgressions,
    and my sin is ever before me.
Against thee, thee only, have I sinned,
    and done that which is evil in thy sight,
so that thou art justified in thy sentence
    and blameless in thy judgment.
Behold, I was brought forth in iniquity,
    and in sin did my mother conceive me.
Behold, thou desirest truth in the inward being;
    therefore teach me wisdom in my secret heart.

Purge me with hyssop, and I shall be clean;
    wash me, and I shall be whiter than snow.
Fill me with joy and gladness;
    let the bones which thou hast broken rejoice.
Hide thy face from my sins,
    and blot out all my iniquities.

Create in me a clean heart, O God,
    and put a new and right spirit within me.
Cast me not away from thy presence,
    and take not thy holy Spirit from me.

Restore to me the joy of thy salvation,
    and uphold me with a willing spirit.

Then I will teach transgressors thy ways,
    and sinners will return to thee.
Deliver me from bloodguiltiness, O God,
    thou God of my salvation,
    and my tongue will sing aloud of thy deliverance.
O Lord, open thou my lips,
    and my mouth shall show forth thy praise.
For thou hast no delight in sacrifice;
    were I to give a burnt offering,
    thou wouldst not be pleased.
The sacrifice acceptable to God is a broken spirit;
    a broken and contrite heart, O God,
    thou wilt not despise.

Do good to Zion in thy good pleasure;
    rebuild the walls of Jerusalem,
then wilt thou delight in right sacrifices,
    in burnt offerings and whole burnt offerings;
    then bulls will be offered on thy altar.

THE FATE OF THE UNGODLY
Psalm 53

The fool says in his heart, 'There is no God.'
    They are corrupt, doing abominable iniquity;
    there is none that does good.

God looks down from heaven
    upon the sons of men
to see if there are any that are wise,
    that seek after God.
They have all fallen away;
    they are all alike depraved;
there is none that does good,
    no, not one.

Have those who work evil no understanding,
     who eat up my people as they eat bread,
     and do not call upon God?
There they are, in great terror,
     in terror such as has not been!
For God will scatter the bones of the ungodly;
     they will be put to shame,
     for God has rejected them.

O that deliverance for Israel would come from Zion!
     When God restores the fortunes of his people,
     Jacob will rejoice and Israel be glad.

THE TREACHERY OF THE WICKED
Psalm 55

Give ear to my prayer, O God;
     and hide not thyself from my supplication!
Attend to me, and answer me;
     I am overcome by my trouble.
I am distraught by the noise of the enemy,
     because of the oppression of the wicked.
For they bring trouble upon me,
     and in anger they cherish enmity against me.

My heart is in anguish within me,
     the terrors of death have fallen upon me.
Fear and trembling come upon me,
     and horror overwhelms me.
And I say, 'O that I had wings like a dove!
     I would fly away and be at rest;
yea, I would wander afar,
     I would lodge in the wilderness,
I would haste to find me a shelter
     from the raging wind and tempest.'

Destroy their plans, O Lord, confuse their tongues;
     for I see violence and strife in the city.

Day and night they go around it on its walls;
    and mischief and trouble are within it,
    ruin is in its midst;
oppression and fraud
    do not depart from its marketplace.

It is not an enemy who taunts me –
    then I could bear it;
it is not an adversary who deals insolently with me –
    then I could hide from him.
But it is you, my equal,
    my companion, my familiar friend.
We used to hold sweet converse together;
    within God's house we walked in fellowship.
Let death come upon them;
    let them go down to Sheol alive;
    let them go away in terror into their graves.

But I call upon God;
    and the Lord will save me.
Evening and morning and at noon
    I utter my complaint and moan,
    and he will hear my voice.
He will deliver my soul in safety
    from the battle that I wage,
    for many are arrayed against me.
God will give ear, and humble them,
    he who is enthroned from of old;
because they keep no law,
    and do not fear God.

My companion stretched out his hand against his friends,
    he violated his covenant.
His speech was smoother than butter,
    yet war was in his heart;
his words were softer than oil,
    yet they were drawn swords.

Cast your burden on the Lord,
and he will sustain you;
he will never permit
the righteous to be moved.
But thou, O God, wilt cast them down
into the lowest pit;
men of blood and treachery
shall not live out half their days.
But I will trust in thee.

CONSUMED BY ZEAL
Psalm 69

Save me, O God!
For the waters have come up to my neck.
I sink in deep mire,
where there is no foothold;
I have come into deep waters,
and the flood sweeps over me.
I am weary with my crying;
my throat is parched.
My eyes grow dim
with waiting for my God.
More in number than the hairs of my head
are those who hate me without cause;
mighty are those who would destroy me,
those who attack me with lies.
What I did not steal
must I now restore?

O God, thou knowest my folly;
the wrongs I have done are not hidden from thee.

Let not those who hope in thee
be put to shame through me,
O Lord God of hosts;

let not those who seek thee
    be brought to dishonour through me,
    O God of Israel.
For it is for thy sake that I have borne reproach,
    that shame has covered my face.
I have become a stranger to my brethren,
    an alien to my mother's sons.
For zeal for thy house has consumed me,
    and the insults of those who insult thee
    have fallen on me.
When I humbled my soul with fasting,
    it became my reproach.
When I made sackcloth my clothing,
    I became a byword to them.
I am the talk of those who sit in the gate,
    and the drunkards make songs about me.

But as for me, my prayer is to thee, O Lord.
    At an acceptable time, O God,
in the abundance of thy steadfast love
    answer me.
With thy faithful help rescue me
    from sinking in the mire;
let me be delivered from my enemies
    and from the deep waters.
Let not the flood sweep over me,
    or the deep swallow me up,
    or the pit close its mouth over me.
Answer me, O Lord, for thy steadfast love is good;
    according to thy abundant mercy, turn to me.
Hide not thy face from thy servant;
    for I am in distress,
    make haste to answer me.
Draw near to me, redeem me,
    set me free because of my enemies!

Thou knowest my reproach,
    and my shame and my dishonour;
    my foes are all known to thee.

Insults have broken my heart,
    so that I am in despair.
I looked for pity, but there was none;
    and for comforters, but I found none.
They gave me poison for food,
    and for my thirst they gave me vinegar to drink.

Let their own table before them become a snare;
    let their sacrificial feasts be a trap.
Let their eyes be darkened, so that they cannot see;
    and make their loins tremble continually.
Pour out thy indignation upon them,
    and let thy burning anger overtake them.
May their camp be a desolation,
    let no one dwell in their tents.
For they persecute him whom thou hast smitten,
    and him whom thou hast wounded,
        they afflict still more.
Add to them punishment upon punishment;
    may they have no acquittal from thee.
Let them be blotted out of the book of the living;
    let them not be enrolled among the righteous.

But I am afflicted and in pain;
    let thy salvation, O God, set me on high!

I will praise the name of God with a song;
    I will magnify him with thanksgiving.
This will please the Lord more than an ox
    or a bull with horns and hoofs.
Let the oppressed see it and be glad;
    you who seek God, let your hearts revive.
For the Lord hears the needy,
    and does not despise his own that are in bonds.

Let heaven and earth praise him,
    the seas and everything that moves therein.

For God will save Zion and rebuild the cities of Judah;
 and his servants shall dwell there and possess it;
the children of his servants shall inherit it,
 and those who love his name shall dwell in it.

HAS GOD FORGOTTEN?
Psalm 77

I cry aloud to God,
 aloud to God, that he may hear me.
In the day of my trouble I seek the Lord;
 in the night my hand is stretched out without wearying;
 my soul refuses to be comforted.

I think of God, and I moan;
 I meditate, and my spirit faints.

Thou dost hold my eyelids from closing;
 I am so troubled that I cannot speak.
I consider the days of old,
 I remember the years long ago.
I commune with my heart in the night;
 I meditate and search my spirit:

'Will the Lord spurn for ever,
 and never again be favorable?
Has his steadfast love for ever ceased?
 Are his promises at an end for all time?
Has God forgotten to be gracious?
 Has he in anger shut up his compassion?'

And I say, 'It is my grief that the right hand
 of the Most High has changed.'
I will call to mind the deeds of the Lord;
 yea, I will remember thy wonders of old.
I will meditate on all thy work,
 and muse on thy mighty deeds.

Thy way, O God, is holy.
    What god is great like our God?
Thou art the God who workest wonders,
    who hast manifested thy might among the peoples.
Thou didst with thy arm redeem thy people,
    the sons of Jacob and Joseph.

When the waters saw thee, O God,
    when the waters saw thee, they were afraid,
    yea, the deep trembled.
The clouds poured out water;
    the skies gave forth thunder;
    thy arrows flashed on every side.
The crash of thy thunder was in the whirlwind;
    thy lightnings lighted up the world;
    the earth trembled and shook.
Thy way was through the sea,
    thy path through the great waters;
    yet thy footprints were unseen.

Thou didst lead thy people like a flock
    by the hand of Moses and Aaron.

CRY FROM THE EDGE OF DARKNESS
Psalm 88

O Lord, my God, I call for help by day;
    I cry out in the night before thee.
Let my prayer come before thee,
    incline thy ear to my cry!

For my soul is full of troubles,
    and my life draws near to Sheol.
I am reckoned among those who go down to the Pit;
    I am a man who has no strength,
like one forsaken among the dead,
    like the slain that lie in the grave,

like those whom thou dost remember no more,
   for they are cut off from thy hand.

Thou hast put me in the depths of the Pit,
   in the regions dark and deep.
Thy wrath lies heavy upon me,
   and thou dost overwhelm me with all thy waves.
Thou hast caused my companions to shun me;
   thou hast made me a thing of horror to them.
I am shut in so that I cannot escape;
   my eye grows dim through sorrow.

Every day I call upon thee, O Lord;
   I spread out my hands to thee.
Dost thou work wonders for the dead?
   Do the shades rise up to praise thee?
Is thy steadfast love declared in the grave,
   or thy faithfulness in Abaddon?
Are thy wonders known in the darkness,
   or thy saving help in the land of forgetfulness?

But I, O Lord, cry to thee;
   in the morning my prayer comes before thee.
O Lord, why dost thou cast me off?
   Why dost thou hide thy face from me?

Afflicted and close to death from my youth up,
   I suffer thy terrors; I am helpless.
Thy wrath has swept over me;
   thy dread assaults destroy me.
They surround me like a flood all day long;
   they close in upon me together.
Thou hast caused lover and friend to shun me;
   my companions are in darkness.

ABANDONED BY GOD
Psalm 102

Hear my prayer, O Lord;
    let my cry come to thee!
Do not hide thy face from me
    in the day of my distress!
Incline thy ear to me;
    answer me speedily in the day when I call!

For my days pass away like smoke,
    and my bones burn like a furnace.
My heart is smitten like grass, and withered;
    I forgot to eat my bread.
Because of my loud groaning
    my bones cleave to my flesh.
I am like a vulture of the wilderness,
    like an owl of the waste places;
I lie awake,
    I am like a lonely bird on the housetop.
All the day my enemies taunt me,
    those who deride me use my name for a curse.
For I eat ashes like bread,
    and mingle tears with my drink,
because of thy indignation and anger;
    for thou hast taken me up and thrown me away.
My days are like an evening shadow;
    I wither away like grass.

But thou, O Lord, art enthroned for ever;
    thy name endures to all generations.
Thou wilt arise and have pity on Zion;
    it is the time to favour her;
    the appointed time has come.

For thy servants hold her stones dear,
    and have pity on her dust.
The nations will fear the name of the Lord,
    and all the kings of the earth thy glory.
For the Lord will build up Zion,
    he will appear in his glory;
he will regard the prayer of the destitute,
    and will not despise their supplication.

Let this be recorded for a generation to come,
    so that a people yet unborn may praise the Lord:
that he looked down from his holy height,
    from heaven the Lord looked at the earth,
to hear the groans of the prisoners,
    to set free those who were doomed to die;
that men may declare in Zion the name of the Lord,
    and in Jerusalem his praise,
when peoples gather together,
    and kingdoms, to worship the Lord.

He has broken my strength in mid-course;
    he has shortened my days.
'O my God,' I say,
    'take me not hence in the midst of my days,
    thou whose years endure throughout all generations!'
Of old thou didst lay the foundation of the earth,
    and the heavens are the work of thy hands.
They will perish, but thou dost endure;
    they will all wear out like a garment.
Thou changest them like raiment, and they pass away;
    but thou art the same, and thy years have no end.
The children of thy servants shall dwell secure;
    their posterity shall be established before thee.

HOPE IN GOD'S FORGIVENESS
Psalm 130

Out of the depths I cry to thee, O Lord!
   Lord, hear my voice!
Let thy ears be attentive
   to the voice of my supplications!

If thou, O Lord, shouldst mark iniquities,
   Lord, who could stand?
But there is forgiveness with thee,
   that thou mayest be feared.
I wait for the Lord, my soul waits,
   and in his word I hope;
my soul waits for the Lord
   more than watchmen for the morning,
   more than watchmen for the morning.

O Israel, hope in the Lord!
   For with the Lord there is steadfast love,
   and with him is plenteous redemption.
And he will redeem Israel
   from all his iniquities.

GOD IS EVERYWHERE
Psalm 139

O Lord, thou hast searched me
   and known me!
Thou knowest when I sit down and when I rise up;
   thou discernest my thoughts from afar.
Thou searchest out my path and my lying down,
   and art acquainted with all my ways.
Even before a word is on my tongue,
   lo, O Lord, thou knowest it altogether.

Thou dost beset me behind and before,
    and layest thy hand upon me.
Such knowledge is too wonderful for me;
    it is high, I cannot attain it.

Whither shall I go from thy Spirit?
    Or whither shall I flee from thy presence?
If I ascend to heaven, thou art there!
    If I make my bed in Sheol, thou art there!
If I take the wings of the morning
    and dwell in the uttermost parts of the sea,
even there thy hand shall lead me,
    and thy right hand shall hold me.

If I say, 'Let only darkness cover me,
    and the light about me be night,'
even the darkness is not dark to thee,
    the night is bright as the day;
    for darkness is as light with thee.

For thou didst form my inward parts,
    thou didst knit me together in my mother's womb.
I praise thee, for thou art fearful and wonderful.
    Wonderful are thy works!
Thou knowest me right well;
    my frame was not hidden from thee,
when I was being made in secret,
    intricately wrought in the depths of the earth.
Thy eyes beheld my unformed substance;
    in thy book were written, every one of them,
the days that were formed for me,
    when as yet there was none of them.

How precious to me are thy thoughts, O God!
    How vast is the sum of them!
If I would count them,
    they are more than the sand.

When I awake,
    I am still with thee.

O that thou wouldst slay the wicked, O God,
    and that men of blood would depart from me,
men who maliciously defy thee,
    who lift themselves up against thee for evil!
Do I not hate them that hate thee, O Lord?
    And do I not loathe them that rise up against thee?
I hate them with perfect hatred;
    I count them my enemies.

Search me, O God, and know my heart!
    Try me and know my thoughts!
And see if there be any wicked way in me,
    and lead me in the way everlasting!

LEAD ME NOT INTO TEMPTATION
Psalm 141

I call upon thee, O Lord; make haste to me!
    Give ear to my voice, when I call to thee!
Let my prayer be counted as incense before thee,
    and the lifting up of my hands as an evening sacrifice!

Set a guard over my mouth, O Lord,
    keep watch over the door of my lips!
Incline not my heart to any evil,
    to busy myself with wicked deeds
in company with men who work iniquity;
    and let me not eat of their dainties!

Let a good man strike or rebuke me in kindness,
    but let the oil of the wicked never anoint my head;
    for my prayer is continually against their wicked deeds.
When they are given over to those who shall condemn them,
    then they shall learn that the word of the Lord is true.

As a rock which one cleaves and shatters on the land,
    so shall their bones be strewn at the mouth of Sheol.

But my eyes are towards thee, O Lord God;
    in thee I seek refuge; leave me not defenceless!
Keep me from the trap which they have laid for me,
    and from the snares of evildoers!
Let the wicked together fall into their own nets,
    while I escape.

DELIVER ME FROM EVIL
Psalm 143

Hear my prayer, O Lord;
    give ear to my supplications!
In thy faithfulness answer me,
    in thy righteousness!
Enter not into judgment with thy servant;
    for no man living is righteous before thee.

For the enemy has pursued me;
    he has crushed my life to the ground;
he has made me sit in darkness
    like those long dead.
Therefore my spirit faints within me;
    my heart within me is appalled.

I remember the days of old,
    I meditate on all that thou hast done;
    I muse on what thy hands have wrought.
I stretch out my hands to thee;
    my soul thirsts for thee like a parched land.

Make haste to answer me, O Lord!
    My spirit fails!
Hide not thy face from me,
    lest I be like those who go down to the Pit.

Let me hear in the morning of thy steadfast love,
    for in thee I put my trust.
Teach me the way I should go,
    for to thee I lift up my soul.
Deliver me, O Lord, from my enemies!
    I have fled to thee for refuge!
Teach me to do thy will,
    for thou art my God!
Let thy good spirit lead me
    on a level path!

For thy name's sake, O Lord, preserve my life!
    In thy righteousness bring me out of trouble!
And in thy steadfast love cut off my enemies,
    and destroy all my adversaries,
        for I am thy servant.

Part Nine

Community Laments

THE DECEIT OF THE WICKED
Psalm 12

Save us, Lord, for no one who is loyal remains;
   good faith between people has vanished.
One lies to another: both talk with smooth words,
   but with duplicity in their hearts.

May the Lord make an end of such smooth words
   and the tongue that talks so boastfully!
They say, 'By our tongues we shall prevail.
   With words as our ally, who can master us?'

'Now I will arise,' says the Lord,
   'for the poor are plundered, the needy groan;
   I shall place them in the safety for which they long.'
The words of the Lord are unalloyed:
   silver refined in a crucible,
   gold purified seven times over.

Lord, you are our protector
   and will for ever guard us from such people.
The wicked parade about,
   and what is of little worth wins general esteem.

A BYWORD AMONG THE NATIONS
Psalm 44

We have heard for ourselves, God,
   our forefathers have told us
what deeds you did in their time,
   all your hand accomplished in days of old.
To plant them in the land, you drove out the nations;
   to settle them, you laid waste the inhabitants.
It was not our fathers' swords that won them the land,
   nor did their strong arm give them victory,
but your right hand and your arm
   and the light of your presence;
   such was your favour to them.

God, you are my King;
   command victory for Jacob.
By your help we shall throw back our enemies,
   in your name we shall trample down our assailants.
My trust is not in my bow,
   nor will my victory be won by my sword;
for you deliver us from our foes,
   you put to confusion those hostile to us.
In God have we gloried all day long,
   and we shall praise your name for ever.

Yet you have rejected and humbled us
   and no longer lead our armies to battle.
You have forced us to retreat before the foe,
   and our enemies have plundered us at will.
You have given us up to be slaughtered like sheep
   and scattered us among the nations.
You sold your people for next to nothing
   and had no profit from the sale.

You have exposed us to the contempt of our neighbours,
   to the gibes and mockery of those about us.

You have made us a byword among the nations,
    and the peoples toss their heads at us;
so all day long my disgrace confronts me,
    and I am covered with shame
at the shouts of those who taunt and abuse me
    as the enemy takes his revenge.

Though all this has befallen us,
    we do not forget you
    and have not been false to your covenant;
our hearts have not been unfaithful,
    nor have our feet strayed from your path.
Yet you have crushed us
    as the sea serpent was crushed,
    and covered us with deepest darkness.
Had we forgotten the name of our God
    and spread our hands in prayer to alien gods,
would not God have found out,
    for he knows the secrets of the heart?
For your sake we are being done to death all day long,
    treated like sheep for slaughter.

Rouse yourself, Lord; why do you sleep?
    Awake! Do not reject us for ever.
Why do you hide your face,
    heedless of our misery and our sufferings?
For we sink down to the dust
    and lie prone on the ground.
Arise and come to our aid;
    for your love's sake deliver us.

A CURSE ON UNJUST RULERS
Psalm 58

You rulers, are your decisions really just?
    Do you judge your people with equity?
No! Your hearts devise wickedness
    and your hands mete out violence in the land.
The wicked go astray from birth:
    liars, no sooner born than they take to wrong ways.
Venomous with the venom of serpents,
    they are like the deaf asp which stops its ears
and will not listen to the sound of the charmer,
    however skilfully he may play.

God, break the teeth in their mouths;
    Lord, shatter the fangs of the oppressors.
May they vanish like water that runs away;
    may he aim his arrows, may they perish by them;
may they be like an abortive birth which melts away
    or a stillborn child which never sees the sun!
Before they know it, may they be rooted up
    like a thorn bush,
    like weeds which a man angrily clears away!
The righteous will rejoice at the sight of vengeance done;
    they will bathe their feet in the blood of the wicked.
It will be said,
    'There is after all reward for the righteous;
    there is after all a God who dispenses justice on earth.'

CRY OF THE DOWNTRODDEN
Psalm 74

God, why have you cast us off?
    And is it for ever?
Why do you fume with anger
    at the flock you used to shepherd?
Remember the assembly of your people,
    taken long since for your own,
    redeemed to be your own tribe.
Remember Mount Zion,
    which you made your dwelling-place.
Restore now what has been altogether ruined,
    all the destruction that the foe has brought on your
        sanctuary.

The shouts of your enemies filled your temple;
    they planted their standards there as tokens of victory.
They brought it crashing down,
    like woodmen plying their axes in the forest;
they ripped out the carvings,
    they smashed them with hatchet and pick.
They set fire to your sanctuary,
    tore down and polluted the abode of your name.
They said to themselves, 'Let us together oppress them,'
    and they burnt every holy place throughout the land.
We cannot see any sign for us,
    we have no prophet now;
    no one amongst us knows how long this is to last.

How long, God, will the foe utter his taunts?
    Will the enemy pour scorn on your name for ever?
Why do you hold back your hand,
    why keep your right hand within your bosom?

God, my King from of old,
    whose saving acts are wrought on earth,
by your power you cleft the sea monster in two
    and broke the sea serpent's heads in the waters;

you crushed the heads of Leviathan
    and threw him to the sharks for food.
You opened channels for spring and torrent;
    you dried up streams never known to fail.
The day is yours, yours also is the night;
    you ordered the light of moon and sun.
You have fixed all the regions of the earth;
    you created both summer and winter.

Remember, Lord, the taunts of the enemy,
    the scorn a barbarous nation pours on your name.
Do not cast to the beasts the soul that confesses you;
    do not forget for ever the sufferings of your servants.
Look upon your creatures:
    they are filled with dark thoughts,
    and the land is a haunt of violence.
Let not the oppressed be shamed and turned away;
    may the poor and the downtrodden praise your name.

Rise up, God, defend your cause;
    remember how fools mock you all day long.
Ignore no longer the uproar of your assailants,
    the ever-rising clamour of those who defy you.

CRY OF THE VANQUISHED
Psalm 79

The heathen have invaded your domain, God;
    they have defiled your holy temple
    and laid Jerusalem in ruins.
The dead bodies of your servants they have thrown out
    as food for the birds;
everyone loyal to you
    they have made carrion for wild beasts.
All round Jerusalem their blood is spilt like water,
    and there is no one to give them burial.

We suffer the taunts of our neighbours,
    the gibes and mockery of those about us.

How long, Lord, will you be roused to such fury?
    How long will your indignation blaze like a fire?
Pour out your wrath on nations that do not acknowledge you,
    on kingdoms that do not call on you by name,
for they have devoured Jacob
    and left his homeland a waste.
Do not remember against us the guilt of past generations;
    rather let your compassion come swiftly to meet us,
    for we have been brought so low.

Help us, God our saviour,
    for the honour of your name;
for your name's sake rescue us
    and wipe out our sins.
Why should the nations ask,
    'Where is their God?'
Before our very eyes may those nations know
    your vengeance for the slaughter of your servants.

Let the groaning of the captives reach your presence
    and in your great might
    save those under sentence of death.
Turn back sevenfold on their own heads, Lord,
    the contempt our neighbours pour on you.
Then we, your people, the flock which you shepherd,
    will give you thanks for ever
    and repeat your praise to all generations.

THE VINE FROM EGYPT
Psalm 80

Hear us, Shepherd of Israel, leading Joseph like a flock.
  Shine forth, as you sit enthroned on the cherubim.
Leading Ephraim, Benjamin, and Manasseh,
  rouse your might and come to our rescue.

God, restore us,
  and make your face shine on us,
  that we may be saved.

Lord God of Hosts,
  how long will you fume at your people's prayer?
You have made sorrow their daily bread
  and copious tears their drink.
You have made us an object of contempt to our neighbours,
  and a laughing-stock to our enemies.
God of Hosts, restore us,
  and make your face shine on us,
  that we may be saved.

You brought a vine from Egypt;
  you drove out nations and planted it;
you cleared the ground for it,
  so that it struck root and filled the land.
The mountains were covered with its shade,
  and its branches were like those of mighty cedars.
It put out boughs all the way to the sea,
  its shoots as far as the river.

Why have you broken down the vineyard wall
  so that every passer-by can pluck its fruit?
The wild boar from the thicket gnaws it,
  and wild creatures of the countryside feed on it.
God of Hosts, turn to us, we pray;
  look down from heaven and see.
Tend this vine,
  this stock which your right hand has planted.

May those who set it on fire and cut it down
    perish before your angry look.
Let your hand rest on the one at your right side,
    the one whom you have made strong for your service.
Then we shall not turn back from you;
    grant us new life, and we shall invoke you by name.

Lord God of Hosts, restore us,
    and make your face shine on us,
    that we may be saved.

GIVE US NEW LIFE
Psalm 85

Lord, you have been gracious to your land
    and turned the tide of Jacob's fortunes.
You have forgiven the guilt of your people
    and put all their sins away.
You have withdrawn all your wrath
    and turned from your hot anger.

God our saviour, restore us
    and abandon your displeasure towards us.
Will you be angry with us for ever?
    Must your wrath last for all generations?
Will you not give us new life
    that your people may rejoice in you?
Lord, show us your love
    and grant us your deliverance.

Let me hear the words of God the Lord:
    he proclaims peace to his people and loyal servants;
    let them not go back to foolish ways.
Deliverance is near to those who worship him,
    so that glory may dwell in our land.
Love and faithfulness have come together;
    justice and peace have embraced.

Faithfulness appears from earth
    and justice looks down from heaven.
The Lord will grant prosperity,
    and our land will yield its harvest.
Justice will go in front of him,
    and peace on the path he treads.

HOW FEW ARE OUR DAYS
Psalm 90

Lord, you have been our refuge
    throughout all generations.
Before the mountains were brought forth
    or the earth and the world were born,
    from age to age you are God.
You turn mortals back to dust,
    saying, 'Turn back, you children of mortals,'
for in your sight a thousand years
    are as the passing of one day
    or as a watch in the night.
You cut them off;
    they are asleep in death.
They are like grass which shoots up;
    though in the morning it flourishes and shoots up,
    by evening it droops and withers.
We are brought to an end by your anger,
    terrified by your wrath.
You set out our iniquities before you,
    our secret sins in the light of your presence.
All our days pass under your wrath;
    our years die away like a murmur.
Seventy years is the span of our life,
    eighty if our strength holds;
at their best they are but toil and sorrow,
    for they pass quickly and we vanish.

Who feels the power of your anger,
    who feels your wrath like those who fear you?
So make us know how few are our days,
    that our minds may learn wisdom.

Lord, how long?
    Turn and show compassion to your servants.
Satisfy us at daybreak with your love,
    that we may sing for joy and be glad all our days.
Grant us days of gladness for the days you have humbled us,
    for the years when we have known misfortune.
May your saving acts appear to your servants,
    and your glory to their children.
May the favour of the Lord our God be on us.
    Establish for us all that we do,
        establish it firmly.

CRY FOR VENGEANCE
Psalm 94

God of vengeance, Lord,
    God of vengeance, show yourself!
Rise, judge of the earth;
    repay the arrogant as they deserve.
Lord, how long will the wicked,
    how long will the wicked exult?
Evildoers are all full of bluster,
    boasting and bragging.
They crush your people, Lord,
    and oppress your chosen nation;
they murder the widow and the stranger
    and put the fatherless to death.
They say, 'The Lord does not see,
    the God of Jacob pays no heed.'

Take heed yourselves, most stupid of people;
    you fools, when will you be wise?
Can he who implanted the ear not hear,
    he who fashioned the eye not see?
Will he who instructs the nations not correct them?
    The teacher of mankind, has he no knowledge?
The Lord knows that the thoughts of everyone
    are but a puff of wind.

Happy the one whom you, Lord, instruct
    and teach from your law,
giving him respite from misfortune
    until a pit is dug for the wicked.
The Lord will not abandon his people
    or forsake his chosen nation;
for justice will again be joined to right,
    and all who are upright in heart will follow it.

Who is on my side against the wicked?
    Who will stand up for me against the evildoers?
Had the Lord not been my helper,
    I should soon have dwelt in the silent grave.
If I said that my foot was slipping,
    your love, Lord, continued to hold me up.
When anxious thoughts filled my heart,
    your comfort brought me joy.

Will corrupt justice win you as an ally,
    contriving mischief under cover of law?
They conspire to take the life of the righteous
    and condemn the innocent to death.
But the Lord has been my strong tower,
    and my God is my rock and refuge.
He will repay the wicked for their injustice;
    the Lord our God will destroy them for their misdeeds.

A CAPTIVE PEOPLE REMEMBERS
Psalm 106

Praise the Lord.

It is good to give thanks to the Lord,
    for his love endures for ever.
Who can tell of the Lord's mighty acts
    and make all his praises heard?
Happy are they who act justly,
    who do what is right at all times!
Remember me, Lord, when you show favour to your people;
    look on me when you save them,
that I may see the prosperity of your chosen ones,
    that I may rejoice in your nation's joy
    and exult with your own people.

Like our forefathers we have sinned,
    we have gone astray and done wrong.
Our forefathers in Egypt disregarded your marvels;
    they were not mindful of your many acts of love,
    and on their journey they rebelled by the Red Sea.
Yet the Lord delivered them for his name's sake
    and so made known his mighty power.
He rebuked the Red Sea, and it dried up;
    he led his people through the deep as through a desert.
He delivered them from those who hated them,
    and rescued them from the enemy's hand.
The waters closed over their adversaries;
    not one of them survived.
Then they believed what he had said
    and sang his praises.

But they soon forgot all he had done
    and would not wait to hear his counsel;
their greed was insatiable in the wilderness,
    there in the desert they tried God's patience.
He gave them what they asked,
    but followed it with a wasting sickness.

In the camp they were envious of Moses,
    and of Aaron, who was consecrated to the Lord.
The earth opened and swallowed Dathan;
    it closed over the company of Abiram.
Fire raged through their company;
    the wicked perished in flames.

At Horeb they made a calf
    and worshipped this image;
they exchanged their God
    for the image of a bull that feeds on grass.
They forgot God their deliverer,
    who had done great things in Egypt,
such marvels in the land of Ham,
    awesome deeds at the Red Sea.
So he purposed to destroy them,
    but Moses, the man he had chosen,
stood before him in the breach
    to prevent his wrath from destroying them.

Disbelieving his promise,
    they rejected the pleasant land.
They muttered treason in their tents,
    and would not obey the Lord.
So with hand uplifted against them he made an oath
    to strike them down in the wilderness,
to scatter their descendants among the nations
    and disperse them throughout the lands.

They joined in worshipping the Baal of Peor
    and ate meat sacrificed to lifeless gods.
Their deeds provoked the Lord to anger,
    and plague broke out amongst them;
but Phinehas stood up and intervened,
    and the plague was checked.
This was counted to him as righteousness
    throughout the generations ever afterwards.

They roused the Lord's anger at the waters of Meribah,
    and it went ill with Moses because of them;
    for when they had embittered his spirit he spoke rashly.

They did not destroy the nations
    as the Lord had commanded them to do,
but they associated with the people
    and learnt their ways;
they worshipped their idols
    and were ensnared by them.
Their sons and their daughters
    they sacrificed to foreign deities;
they shed innocent blood,
    the blood of sons and daughters
offered to the gods of Canaan,
    and the land was polluted with blood.
Thus they defiled themselves by their actions
    and were faithless in their conduct.

Then the Lord became angry with his people and,
    though they were his own chosen nation, he loathed them;
he handed them over to the nations,
    and they were ruled by their foes;
their enemies oppressed them
    and kept them in subjection to their power.
Time and again he came to their rescue,
    but they were rebellious in their designs,
    and so were brought low by their wrongdoing.
Yet when he heard them wail and cry aloud
    he looked with pity on their distress;
he called to mind his covenant with them
    and, in his boundless love, relented;
he roused compassion for them
    in the hearts of all their captors.

Deliver us, Lord our God,
    and gather us in from among the nations,
that we may give thanks to your holy name
    and make your praise our pride.

HOPE FOR THE HARVEST
Psalm 126

When the Lord restored the fortunes of Zion,
  we were like people renewed in health.
Our mouths were full of laughter
  and our tongues sang aloud for joy.
Then among the nations it was said,
  'The Lord has done great things for them.'
Great things indeed the Lord did for us,
  and we rejoiced.

Restore our fortunes, Lord,
  as streams return in the Negeb.
Those who sow in tears
  will reap with songs of joy.
He who goes out weeping,
  carrying his bag of seed,
will come back with songs of joy,
  carrying home his sheaves.

SONG OF THE EXILED
Psalm 137

By the rivers of Babylon we sat down and wept
  as we remembered Zion.
On the willow trees there
  we hung up our lyres,
for there those who had carried us captive
  asked us to sing them a song,
our captors called on us to be joyful:
  'Sing us one of the songs of Zion.'

How could we sing the Lord's song
  in a foreign land?
If I forget you, Jerusalem,
  may my right hand wither away;

let my tongue cling to the roof of my mouth
    if I do not remember you,
    if I do not set Jerusalem above my chief joy.

Remember, Lord, against the Edomites
    the day when Jerusalem fell,
how they shouted, 'Down with it, down with it,
    down to its very foundations!'

Babylon, Babylon the destroyer,
    happy is he who repays you
    for what you did to us!
Happy is he who seizes your babes
    and dashes them against a rock.

Part Ten

Wisdom Psalms

SPIRITUAL GROWTH
Psalm 1

Happy are those
who do not follow the advice of the wicked,
or take the path that sinners tread,
or sit in the seat of scoffers;
but their delight is in the law of the Lord,
and on his law they meditate day and night.
They are like trees planted by streams of water,
which yield their fruit in its season,
and their leaves do not wither.
In all that they do, they prosper.

The wicked are not so,
but are like chaff that the wind drives away.
Therefore the wicked will not stand in the judgment,
nor sinners in the congregation of the righteous;
for the Lord watches over the way of the righteous,
but the way of the wicked will perish.

THE FOUNTAIN OF LIFE
Psalm 36

Transgression speaks to the wicked
    deep in their hearts;
there is no fear of God
    before their eyes.
For they flatter themselves in their own eyes
    that their iniquity cannot be found out and hated.
The words of their mouths are mischief and deceit;
    they have ceased to act wisely and do good.
They plot mischief while on their beds;
    they are set on a way that is not good;
    they do not reject evil.

Your steadfast love, O Lord, extends to the heavens,
    your faithfulness to the clouds.
Your righteousness is like the mighty mountains,
    your judgments are like the great deep;
    you save humans and animals alike, O Lord.
How precious is your steadfast love, O God!
    All people may take refuge in the shadow of your wings.
They feast on the abundance of your house,
    and you give them drink from the river of your delights.
For with you is the fountain of life;
    in your light we see light.

O continue your steadfast love to those who know you,
    and your salvation to the upright of heart!
Do not let the foot of the arrogant tread on me,
    or the hand of the wicked drive me away.
There the evildoers lie prostrate;
    they are thrust down, unable to rise.

WAIT PATIENTLY FOR GOD
Psalm 37

Do not fret because of the wicked;
  do not be envious of wrongdoers,
for they will soon fade like the grass,
  and wither like the green herb.

Trust in the Lord, and do good;
  so you will live in the land, and enjoy security.
Take delight in the Lord,
  and he will give you the desires of your heart.

Commit your way to the Lord;
  trust in him, and he will act.
He will make your vindication shine like the light,
  and the justice of your cause like the noonday.

Be still before the Lord, and wait patiently for him;
  do not fret over those who prosper in their way,
  over those who carry out evil devices.

Refrain from anger, and forsake wrath.
  Do not fret – it leads only to evil.
For the wicked shall be cut off,
  but those who wait for the Lord shall inherit the land.

Yet a little while, and the wicked will be no more;
  though you look diligently for their place,
  they will not be there.
But the meek shall inherit the land,
  and delight in abundant prosperity.

The wicked plot against the righteous,
  and gnash their teeth at them;
but the Lord laughs at the wicked,
  for he sees that their day is coming.

The wicked draw the sword
  and bend their bows

to bring down the poor and needy,
    to kill those who walk uprightly;
their sword shall enter their own heart,
    and their bows shall be broken.

Better is a little that the righteous person has
    than the abundance of many wicked.
For the arms of the wicked shall be broken,
    but the Lord upholds the righteous.

The Lord knows the days of the blameless,
    and their heritage will abide for ever;
they are not put to shame in evil times,
    in the days of famine they have abundance.

But the wicked perish,
    and the enemies of the Lord are like the glory of
        the pastures;
    they vanish – like smoke they vanish away.
The wicked borrow, and do not pay back,
    but the righteous are generous and keep giving;
for those blessed by the Lord shall inherit the land,
    but those cursed by him shall be cut off.

Our steps are made firm by the Lord,
    when he delights in our way;
though we stumble, we shall not fall headlong,
    for the Lord holds us by the hand.

I have been young, and now am old,
    yet I have not seen the righteous forsaken
    or their children begging bread.
They are ever giving liberally and lending,
    and their children become a blessing.

Depart from evil, and do good;
    so you shall abide for ever.
For the Lord loves justice;
    he will not forsake his faithful ones.

The righteous shall be kept safe for ever,
  but the children of the wicked shall be cut off.
The righteous shall inherit the land,
  and live in it for ever.

The mouths of the righteous utter wisdom,
  and their tongues speak justice.
The law of their God is in their hearts;
  their steps do not slip.

The wicked watch for the righteous,
  and seek to kill them.
The Lord will not abandon them to their power,
  or let them be condemned when they are brought to trial.

Wait for the Lord, and keep to his way,
  and he will exalt you to inherit the land;
  you will look on the destruction of the wicked.

I have seen the wicked oppressing,
  and towering like a cedar of Lebanon.
Again I passed by, and they were no more;
  though I sought them, they could not be found.

Mark the blameless, and behold the upright,
  for there is posterity for the peaceable.
But transgressors shall be altogether destroyed;
  the posterity of the wicked shall be cut off.

The salvation of the righteous is from the Lord;
  he is their refuge in the time of trouble.
The Lord helps them and rescues them;
  he rescues them from the wicked, and saves them,
  because they take refuge in him.

THE USELESSNESS OF RICHES
Psalm 49

Hear this, all you peoples;
  give ear, all inhabitants of the world,
both low and high,
  rich and poor together.
My mouth shall speak wisdom;
  the meditation of my heart shall be understanding.
I will incline my ear to a proverb;
  I will solve my riddle to the music of the harp.
Why should I fear in times of trouble,
  when the iniquity of my persecutors surrounds me,
those who trust in their wealth
  and boast of the abundance of their riches?
Truly, no ransom avails for one's life,
  there is no price one can give to God for it.
For the ransom of life is costly,
  and can never suffice,
that one should live on for ever
  and never see the grave.

When we look at the wise, they die;
  fool and dolt perish together
  and leave their wealth to others.
Their graves are their homes for ever,
  their dwelling-places to all generations,
  though they named lands their own.

Mortals cannot abide in their pomp;
  they are like the animals that perish.

Such is the fate of the foolhardy,
  the end of those who are pleased with their lot.
Like sheep they are appointed for Sheol;
  Death shall be their shepherd;
straight to the grave they descend,
  and their form shall waste away;

172

Sheol shall be their home.
But God will ransom my soul from the power of Sheol,
    for he will receive me.

Do not be afraid when some become rich,
    when the wealth of their houses increases.
For when they die they will carry nothing away;
    their wealth will not go down after them.
Though in their lifetime they count themselves happy –
    for you are praised when you do well for yourself –
they will go to the company of their ancestors,
    who will never again see the light.

Mortals cannot abide in their pomp;
    they are like the animals that perish.

MY HEART'S DESIRE
Psalm 73

Truly God is good to the upright,
    to those who are pure in heart.

But as for me, my feet had almost stumbled;
    my steps had nearly slipped.
For I was envious of the arrogant;
    I saw the prosperity of the wicked.

For they have no pain;
    their bodies are sound and sleek.
They are not in trouble as others are;
    they are not plagued like other people.
Therefore pride is their necklace;
    violence covers them like a garment.
Their eyes swell out with fatness;
    their hearts overflow with follies.
They scoff and speak with malice;
    loftily they threaten oppression.

They set their mouths against heaven,
    and their tongues range over the earth.
Therefore the people turn and praise them,
    and find no fault in them.
And they say, 'How can God know?
    Is there knowledge in the Most High?'

Such are the wicked;
    always at ease, they increase in riches.
All in vain I have kept my heart clean
    and washed my hands in innocence.
For all day long I have been plagued,
    and am punished every morning.

If I had said, 'I will talk on in this way',
    I would have been untrue to the circle of your children.
But when I thought how to understand this,
    it seemed to me a wearisome task,
until I went into the sanctuary of God;
    then I perceived their end.

Truly you set them in slippery places;
    you make them fall to ruin.
How they are destroyed in a moment,
    swept away utterly by terrors!
They are like a dream when one awakes;
    on awaking you despise their phantoms.

When my soul was embittered,
    when I was pricked in heart,
I was stupid and ignorant;
    I was like a brute beast towards you.

Nevertheless I am continually with you;
    you hold my right hand.
You guide me with your counsel,
    and afterwards you will receive me with honour.
Whom have I in heaven but you?
    And there is nothing on earth that I desire other than you.

My flesh and my heart may fail,
  but God is the strength of my heart
  and my portion for ever.

Indeed, those who are far from you will perish;
  you put an end to those who are false to you.
But for me it is good to be near God;
  I have made the Lord God my refuge,
  to tell of all your works.

DELIGHT IN GOD'S LAW
Psalm 119

Happy are those whose way is blameless,
  who walk in the law of the Lord.
Happy are those who keep his decrees,
  who seek him with their whole heart,
who also do no wrong,
  but walk in his ways.
You have commanded your precepts
  to be kept diligently.
O that my ways may be steadfast
  in keeping your statutes!
Then I shall not be put to shame,
  having my eyes fixed on all your commandments.
I will praise you with an upright heart,
  when I learn your righteous ordinances.
I will observe your statutes;
  do not utterly forsake me.

How can young people keep their way pure?
  By guarding it according to your word.
With my whole heart I seek you;
  do not let me stray from your commandments.
I treasure your word in my heart,
  so that I may not sin against you.

Blessed are you, O Lord;
    teach me your statutes.
With my lips I declare
    all the ordinances of your mouth.
I delight in the way of your decrees
    as much as in all riches.
I will meditate on your precepts,
    and fix my eyes on your ways.
I will delight in your statutes;
    I will not forget your word.

Deal bountifully with your servant,
    so that I may live and observe your word.
Open my eyes, so that I may behold
    wondrous things out of your law.
I live as an alien in the land;
    do not hide your commandments from me.
My soul is consumed with longing
    for your ordinances at all times.
You rebuke the insolent, accursed ones,
    who wander from your commandments;
take away from me their scorn and contempt,
    for I have kept your decrees.
Even though princes sit plotting against me,
    your servant will meditate on your statutes.
Your decrees are my delight,
    they are my counsellors.

My soul clings to the dust;
    revive me according to your word.
When I told of my ways, you answered me;
    teach me your statutes.
Make me understand the way of your precepts,
    and I will meditate on your wondrous works.
My soul melts away for sorrow;
    strengthen me according to your word.
Put false ways far from me;
    and graciously teach me your law.

I have chosen the way of faithfulness;
  I set your ordinances before me.
I cling to your decrees, O Lord;
  let me not be put to shame.
I run the way of your commandments,
  for you enlarge my understanding.

Teach me, O Lord, the way of your statutes,
  and I will observe it to the end.
Give me understanding, that I may keep your law
  and observe it with my whole heart.
Lead me in the path of your commandments,
  for I delight in it.
Turn my heart to your decrees,
  and not to selfish gain.
Turn my eyes from looking at vanities;
  give me life in your ways.
Confirm to your servant your promise,
  which is for those who fear you.
Turn away the disgrace that I dread,
  for your ordinances are good.
See, I have longed for your precepts;
  in your righteousness give me life.

Let your steadfast love come to me, O Lord,
  your salvation according to your promise.
Then I shall have an answer for those who taunt me,
  for I trust in your word.
Do not take the word of truth utterly out of my mouth,
  for my hope is in your ordinances.
I will keep your law continually,
  for ever and ever.
I shall walk at liberty,
  for I have sought your precepts.
I will also speak of your decrees before kings,
  and shall not be put to shame;
I find my delight in your commandments,
  because I love them.

I revere your commandments, which I love,
    and I will meditate on your statutes.

Remember your word to your servant,
    in which you have made me hope.
This is my comfort in my distress,
    that your promise gives me life.
The arrogant utterly deride me,
    but I do not turn away from your law.
When I think of your ordinances from of old,
    I take comfort, O Lord.
Hot indignation seizes me because of the wicked,
    those who forsake your law.
Your statutes have been my songs
    wherever I make my home.
I remember your name in the night, O Lord,
    and keep your law.
This blessing has fallen to me,
    for I have kept your precepts.

The Lord is my portion;
    I promise to keep your words.
I implore your favour with all my heart;
    be gracious to me according to your promise.
When I think of your ways,
    I turn my feet to your decrees;
I hurry and do not delay
    to keep your commandments.
Though the cords of the wicked ensnare me,
    I do not forget your law.
At midnight I rise to praise you,
    because of your righteous ordinances.
I am a companion of all who fear you,
    of those who keep your precepts.
The earth, O Lord, is full of your steadfast love;
    teach me your statutes.

You have dealt well with your servant, O Lord,
    according to your word.
Teach me good judgment and knowledge,
    for I believe in your commandments.
Before I was humbled I went astray,
    but now I keep your word.
You are good and do good;
    teach me your statutes.
The arrogant smear me with lies,
    but with my whole heart I keep your precepts.
Their hearts are fat and gross,
    but I delight in your law.
It is good for me that I was humbled,
    so that I might learn your statutes.
The law of your mouth is better to me
    than thousands of gold and silver pieces.

Your hands have made and fashioned me;
    give me understanding that I may learn your commandments.
Those who fear you shall see me and rejoice,
    because I have hoped in your word.
I know, O Lord, that your judgments are right,
    and that in faithfulness you have humbled me.
Let your steadfast love become my comfort
    according to your promise to your servant.
Let your mercy come to me, that I may live;
    for your law is my delight.
Let the arrogant be put to shame,
    because they have subverted me with guile;
    as for me, I will meditate on your precepts.
Let those who fear you turn to me,
    so that they may know your decrees.
May my heart be blameless in your statutes,
    so that I may not be put to shame.

My soul languishes for your salvation;
    I hope in your word.

My eyes fail with watching for your promise;
    I ask, 'When will you comfort me?'
For I have become like a wineskin in the smoke,
    yet I have not forgotten your statutes.
How long must your servant endure?
    When will you judge those who persecute me?
The arrogant have dug pitfalls for me;
    they flout your law.
All your commandments are enduring;
    I am persecuted without cause; help me!
They have almost made an end of me on earth;
    but I have not forsaken your precepts.
In your steadfast love spare my life,
    so that I may keep the decrees of your mouth.

The Lord exists for ever;
    your word is firmly fixed in heaven.
Your faithfulness endures to all generations;
    you have established the earth, and it stands fast.
By your appointment they stand today,
    for all things are your servants.
If your law had not been my delight,
    I would have perished in my misery.
I will never forget your precepts,
    for by them you have given me life.
I am yours; save me,
    for I have sought your precepts.
The wicked lie in wait to destroy me,
    but I consider your decrees.
I have seen a limit to all perfection,
    but your commandment is exceedingly broad.

Oh, how I love your law!
    It is my meditation all day long.
Your commandment makes me wiser than my enemies,
    for it is always with me.
I have more understanding than all my teachers,
    for your decrees are my meditation.

I understand more than the aged,
 for I keep your precepts.
I hold back my feet from every evil way,
 in order to keep your word.
I do not turn away from your ordinances,
 for you have taught me.
How sweet are your words to my taste,
 sweeter than honey to my mouth!
Through your precepts I get understanding;
 therefore I hate every false way.

Your word is a lamp to my feet
 and a light to my path.
I have sworn an oath and confirmed it,
 to observe your righteous ordinances.
I am severely afflicted;
 give me life, O Lord, according to your word.
Accept my offerings of praise, O Lord,
 and teach me your ordinances.
I hold my life in my hand continually,
 but I do not forget your law.
The wicked have laid a snare for me,
 but I do not stray from your precepts.
Your decrees are my heritage for ever;
 they are the joy of my heart.
I incline my heart to perform your statutes
 for ever, to the end.

I hate the double-minded,
 but I love your law.
You are my hiding-place and my shield;
 I hope in your word.
Go away from me, you evildoers,
 that I may keep the commandments of my God.
Uphold me according to your promise, that I may live,
 and let me not be put to shame in my hope.
Hold me up, that I may be safe
 and have regard for your statutes continually.

You spurn all who go astray from your statutes;
    for their cunning is in vain.
All the wicked of the earth you count as dross;
    therefore I love your decrees.
My flesh trembles for fear of you,
    and I am afraid of your judgments.

I have done what is just and right;
    do not leave me to my oppressors.
Guarantee your servant's well-being;
    do not let the godless oppress me.
My eyes fail from watching for your salvation,
    and for the fulfilment of your righteous promise.
Deal with your servant according to your steadfast love,
    and teach me your statutes.
I am your servant; give me understanding,
    so that I may know your decrees.
It is time for the Lord to act,
    for your law has been broken.
Truly I love your commandments
    more than gold, more than fine gold.
Truly I direct my steps by all your precepts;
    I hate every false way.

Your decrees are wonderful;
    therefore my soul keeps them.
The unfolding of your words gives light;
    it imparts understanding to the simple.
With open mouth I pant,
    because I long for your commandments.
Turn to me and be gracious to me,
    as is your custom towards those who love your name.
Keep my steps steady according to your promise,
    and never let iniquity have dominion over me.
Redeem me from human oppression,
    that I may keep your precepts.
Make your face shine upon your servant,
    and teach me your statutes.

My eyes shed streams of tears
    because your law is not kept.

You are righteous, O Lord,
    and your judgments are right.
You have appointed your decrees in righteousness
    and in all faithfulness.
My zeal consumes me
    because my foes forget your words.
Your promise is well tried,
    and your servant loves it.
I am small and despised,
    yet I do not forget your precepts.
Your righteousness is an everlasting righteousness,
    and your law is the truth.
Trouble and anguish have come upon me,
    but your commandments are my delight.
Your decrees are righteous for ever;
    give me understanding that I may live.

With my whole heart I cry; answer me, O Lord.
    I will keep your statutes.
I cry to you; save me,
    that I may observe your decrees.
I rise before dawn and cry for help;
    I put my hope in your words.
My eyes are awake before each watch of the night,
    that I may meditate on your promise.
In your steadfast love hear my voice;
    O Lord, in your justice preserve my life.
Those who persecute me with evil purpose draw near;
    they are far from your law.
Yet you are near, O Lord,
    and all your commandments are true.
Long ago I learned from your decrees
    that you have established them for ever.

Look on my misery and rescue me,
    for I do not forget your law.
Plead my cause and redeem me;
    give me life according to your promise.
Salvation is far from the wicked,
    for they do not seek your statutes.
Great is your mercy, O Lord;
    give me life according to your justice.
Many are my persecutors and my adversaries,
    yet I do not swerve from your decrees.
I look at the faithless with disgust,
    because they do not keep your commands.
Consider how I love your precepts;
    preserve my life according to your steadfast love.
The sum of your word is truth;
    and every one of your righteous ordinances endures for ever.

Princes persecute me without cause,
    but my heart stands in awe of your words.
I rejoice at your word
    like one who finds great spoil.
I hate and abhor falsehood,
    but I love your law.
Seven times a day I praise you
    for your righteous ordinances.
Great peace have those who love your law;
    nothing can make them stumble.
I hope for your salvation, O Lord,
    and I fulfil your commandments.
My soul keeps your decrees;
    I love them exceedingly.
I keep your precepts and decrees,
    for all my ways are before you.

Let my cry come before you, O Lord;
    give me understanding according to your word.
Let my supplication come before you;
    deliver me according to your promise.

My lips will pour forth praise,
    because you teach me your statutes.
My tongue will sing of your promise,
    for all your commandments are right.
Let your hand be ready to help me,
    for I have chosen your precepts.
I long for your salvation, O Lord,
    and your law is my delight.
Let me live that I may praise you,
    and let your ordinances help me.
I have gone astray like a lost sheep;
    seek out your servant,
        for I do not forget your commandments.

A HERITAGE FROM THE LORD
Psalm 127

Unless the Lord builds the house,
    those who build it labour in vain.
Unless the Lord guards the city,
    the guard keeps watch in vain.
It is in vain that you rise up early
    and go late to rest,
eating the bread of anxious toil;
    for he gives sleep to his beloved.

Sons are indeed a heritage from the Lord,
    the fruit of the womb a reward.
Like arrows in the hand of a warrior
    are the sons of one's youth.
Happy is the man who has
    his quiver full of them.
He shall not be put to shame
    when he speaks with his enemies in the gate.

THE LORD'S BLESSING
Psalm 133

How very good and pleasant it is
    when kindred live together in unity!
It is like the precious oil on the head,
    running down upon the beard,
on the beard of Aaron,
    running down over the collar of his robes.
It is like the dew of Hermon,
    which falls on the mountains of Zion.
For there the Lord ordained his blessing,
    life for evermore.

Index of Psalms

Index of Primary Sources